T0289823

THIS IS YOUR **PASSBOOK**® FOR ...

DATA ENTRY SUPERVISOR

NATIONAL LEARNING CORPORATION®

passbooks.com

COPYRIGHT NOTICE

Copyright © 2022 by

National Learning Corporation

212 Michael Drive, Syosset, NY 11791
(516) 921-8888 • www.passbooks.com
E-mail: info@passbooks.com

PUBLISHED IN THE UNITED STATES OF AMERICA

PASSBOOK® SERIES

THE *PASSBOOK® SERIES* has been created to prepare applicants and candidates for the ultimate academic battlefield – the examination room.

At some time in our lives, each and every one of us may be required to take an examination – for validation, matriculation, admission, qualification, registration, certification, or licensure.

Based on the assumption that every applicant or candidate has met the basic formal educational standards, has taken the required number of courses, and read the necessary texts, the *PASSBOOK® SERIES* furnishes the one special preparation which may assure passing with confidence, instead of failing with insecurity. Examination questions – together with answers – are furnished as the basic vehicle for study so that the mysteries of the examination and its compounding difficulties may be eliminated or diminished by a sure method.

This book is meant to help you pass your examination provided that you qualify and are serious in your objective.

The entire field is reviewed through the huge store of content information which is succinctly presented through a provocative and challenging approach – the question-and-answer method.

A climate of success is established by furnishing the correct answers at the end of each test.

You soon learn to recognize types of questions, forms of questions, and patterns of questioning. You may even begin to anticipate expected outcomes.

You perceive that many questions are repeated or adapted so that you can gain acute insights, which may enable you to score many sure points.

You learn how to confront new questions, or types of questions, and to attack them confidently and work out the correct answers.

You note objectives and emphases, and recognize pitfalls and dangers, so that you may make positive educational adjustments.

Moreover, you are kept fully informed in relation to new concepts, methods, practices, and directions in the field.

You discover that you arre actually taking the examination all the time: you are preparing for the examination by "taking" an examination, not by reading extraneous and/or supererogatory textbooks.

In short, this PASSBOOK®, used directedly, should be an important factor in helping you to pass your test.

DATA ENTRY SUPERVISOR

DUTIES
    Supervises the operation of data entry equipment and operators including their orientation, training, counseling, evaluation and discipline in accordance with departmental standards; assigns duties and reviews results for accuracy, effectiveness and conformance with policy; studies, analyzes and evaluates the tasks performed by unit; prepares production schedule, assigning work and keeping time and production records; reviews work for accuracy; instructs trainees in equipment operation; acts as assistant supervisor in a large data entry installation; does related work as required.

SCOPE OF THE EXAMINATION
The written test will be designed to cover knowledges in the following areas:
1. Considerable skill in operating data entry and related equipment;
2. Knowledge of the applications, functions and procedures related to the area and specific equipment;
3. Knowledge of electronic data processing, including storage/retrieval and input/output media;
4. Ability to give and follow complex written and oral instructions;
5. Communication skills;
6. Clerical aptitude;
7. Ability to maintain records; and
8. Supervisory ability.

HOW TO TAKE A TEST

I. YOU MUST PASS AN EXAMINATION

A. *WHAT EVERY CANDIDATE SHOULD KNOW*

Examination applicants often ask us for help in preparing for the written test. What can I study in advance? What kinds of questions will be asked? How will the test be given? How will the papers be graded?

As an applicant for a civil service examination, you may be wondering about some of these things. Our purpose here is to suggest effective methods of advance study and to describe civil service examinations.

Your chances for success on this examination can be increased if you know how to prepare. Those "pre-examination jitters" can be reduced if you know what to expect. You can even experience an adventure in good citizenship if you know why civil service exams are given.

B. *WHY ARE CIVIL SERVICE EXAMINATIONS GIVEN?*

Civil service examinations are important to you in two ways. As a citizen, you want public jobs filled by employees who know how to do their work. As a job seeker, you want a fair chance to compete for that job on an equal footing with other candidates. The best-known means of accomplishing this two-fold goal is the competitive examination.

Exams are widely publicized throughout the nation. They may be administered for jobs in federal, state, city, municipal, town or village governments or agencies.

Any citizen may apply, with some limitations, such as the age or residence of applicants. Your experience and education may be reviewed to see whether you meet the requirements for the particular examination. When these requirements exist, they are reasonable and applied consistently to all applicants. Thus, a competitive examination may cause you some uneasiness now, but it is your privilege and safeguard.

C. *HOW ARE CIVIL SERVICE EXAMS DEVELOPED?*

Examinations are carefully written by trained technicians who are specialists in the field known as "psychological measurement," in consultation with recognized authorities in the field of work that the test will cover. These experts recommend the subject matter areas or skills to be tested; only those knowledges or skills important to your success on the job are included. The most reliable books and source materials available are used as references. Together, the experts and technicians judge the difficulty level of the questions.

Test technicians know how to phrase questions so that the problem is clearly stated. Their ethics do not permit "trick" or "catch" questions. Questions may have been tried out on sample groups, or subjected to statistical analysis, to determine their usefulness.

Written tests are often used in combination with performance tests, ratings of training and experience, and oral interviews. All of these measures combine to form the best-known means of finding the right person for the right job.

II. HOW TO PASS THE WRITTEN TEST

A. NATURE OF THE EXAMINATION

To prepare intelligently for civil service examinations, you should know how they differ from school examinations you have taken. In school you were assigned certain definite pages to read or subjects to cover. The examination questions were quite detailed and usually emphasized memory. Civil service exams, on the other hand, try to discover your present ability to perform the duties of a position, plus your potentiality to learn these duties. In other words, a civil service exam attempts to predict how successful you will be. Questions cover such a broad area that they cannot be as minute and detailed as school exam questions.

In the public service similar kinds of work, or positions, are grouped together in one "class." This process is known as *position-classification*. All the positions in a class are paid according to the salary range for that class. One class title covers all of these positions, and they are all tested by the same examination.

B. FOUR BASIC STEPS

1) Study the announcement

How, then, can you know what subjects to study? Our best answer is: "Learn as much as possible about the class of positions for which you've applied." The exam will test the knowledge, skills and abilities needed to do the work.

Your most valuable source of information about the position you want is the official exam announcement. This announcement lists the training and experience qualifications. Check these standards and apply only if you come reasonably close to meeting them.

The brief description of the position in the examination announcement offers some clues to the subjects which will be tested. Think about the job itself. Review the duties in your mind. Can you perform them, or are there some in which you are rusty? Fill in the blank spots in your preparation.

Many jurisdictions preview the written test in the exam announcement by including a section called "Knowledge and Abilities Required," "Scope of the Examination," or some similar heading. Here you will find out specifically what fields will be tested.

2) Review your own background

Once you learn in general what the position is all about, and what you need to know to do the work, ask yourself which subjects you already know fairly well and which need improvement. You may wonder whether to concentrate on improving your strong areas or on building some background in your fields of weakness. When the announcement has specified "some knowledge" or "considerable knowledge," or has used adjectives like "beginning principles of…" or "advanced … methods," you can get a clue as to the number and difficulty of questions to be asked in any given field. More questions, and hence broader coverage, would be included for those subjects which are more important in the work. Now weigh your strengths and weaknesses against the job requirements and prepare accordingly.

3) Determine the level of the position

Another way to tell how intensively you should prepare is to understand the level of the job for which you are applying. Is it the entering level? In other words, is this the position in which beginners in a field of work are hired? Or is it an intermediate or advanced level? Sometimes this is indicated by such words as "Junior" or "Senior" in the class title. Other jurisdictions use Roman numerals to designate the level – Clerk I, Clerk II, for example. The word "Supervisor" sometimes appears in the title. If the level is not indicated by the title, check the description of duties. Will you be working under very close supervision, or will you have responsibility for independent decisions in this work?

4) Choose appropriate study materials

Now that you know the subjects to be examined and the relative amount of each subject to be covered, you can choose suitable study materials. For beginning level jobs, or even advanced ones, if you have a pronounced weakness in some aspect of your training, read a modern, standard textbook in that field. Be sure it is up to date and has general coverage. Such books are normally available at your library, and the librarian will be glad to help you locate one. For entry-level positions, questions of appropriate difficulty are chosen – neither highly advanced questions, nor those too simple. Such questions require careful thought but not advanced training.

If the position for which you are applying is technical or advanced, you will read more advanced, specialized material. If you are already familiar with the basic principles of your field, elementary textbooks would waste your time. Concentrate on advanced textbooks and technical periodicals. Think through the concepts and review difficult problems in your field.

These are all general sources. You can get more ideas on your own initiative, following these leads. For example, training manuals and publications of the government agency which employs workers in your field can be useful, particularly for technical and professional positions. A letter or visit to the government department involved may result in more specific study suggestions, and certainly will provide you with a more definite idea of the exact nature of the position you are seeking.

III. KINDS OF TESTS

Tests are used for purposes other than measuring knowledge and ability to perform specified duties. For some positions, it is equally important to test ability to make adjustments to new situations or to profit from training. In others, basic mental abilities not dependent on information are essential. Questions which test these things may not appear as pertinent to the duties of the position as those which test for knowledge and information. Yet they are often highly important parts of a fair examination. For very general questions, it is almost impossible to help you direct your study efforts. What we can do is to point out some of the more common of these general abilities needed in public service positions and describe some typical questions.

1) General information

Broad, general information has been found useful for predicting job success in some kinds of work. This is tested in a variety of ways, from vocabulary lists to questions about current events. Basic background in some field of work, such as sociology or economics, may be sampled in a group of questions. Often these are principles which have become familiar to most persons through exposure rather than through formal training. It is difficult to advise you how to study for these questions; being alert to the world around you is our best suggestion.

2) Verbal ability

An example of an ability needed in many positions is verbal or language ability. Verbal ability is, in brief, the ability to use and understand words. Vocabulary and grammar tests are typical measures of this ability. Reading comprehension or paragraph interpretation questions are common in many kinds of civil service tests. You are given a paragraph of written material and asked to find its central meaning.

3) Numerical ability

Number skills can be tested by the familiar arithmetic problem, by checking paired lists of numbers to see which are alike and which are different, or by interpreting charts and graphs. In the latter test, a graph may be printed in the test booklet which you are asked to use as the basis for answering questions.

4) Observation

A popular test for law-enforcement positions is the observation test. A picture is shown to you for several minutes, then taken away. Questions about the picture test your ability to observe both details and larger elements.

5) Following directions

In many positions in the public service, the employee must be able to carry out written instructions dependably and accurately. You may be given a chart with several columns, each column listing a variety of information. The questions require you to carry out directions involving the information given in the chart.

6) Skills and aptitudes

Performance tests effectively measure some manual skills and aptitudes. When the skill is one in which you are trained, such as typing or shorthand, you can practice. These tests are often very much like those given in business school or high school courses. For many of the other skills and aptitudes, however, no short-time preparation can be made. Skills and abilities natural to you or that you have developed throughout your lifetime are being tested.

Many of the general questions just described provide all the data needed to answer the questions and ask you to use your reasoning ability to find the answers. Your best preparation for these tests, as well as for tests of facts and ideas, is to be at your physical and mental best. You, no doubt, have your own methods of getting into an exam-taking mood and keeping "in shape." The next section lists some ideas on this subject.

IV. KINDS OF QUESTIONS

Only rarely is the "essay" question, which you answer in narrative form, used in civil service tests. Civil service tests are usually of the short-answer type. Full instructions for answering these questions will be given to you at the examination. But in case this is your first experience with short-answer questions and separate answer sheets, here is what you need to know:

1) Multiple-choice Questions

Most popular of the short-answer questions is the "multiple choice" or "best answer" question. It can be used, for example, to test for factual knowledge, ability to solve problems or judgment in meeting situations found at work.

A multiple-choice question is normally one of three types—

- It can begin with an incomplete statement followed by several possible endings. You are to find the one ending which *best* completes the statement, although some of the others may not be entirely wrong.
- It can also be a complete statement in the form of a question which is answered by choosing one of the statements listed.
- It can be in the form of a problem – again you select the best answer.

Here is an example of a multiple-choice question with a discussion which should give you some clues as to the method for choosing the right answer:

When an employee has a complaint about his assignment, the action which will *best* help him overcome his difficulty is to
   A. discuss his difficulty with his coworkers
   B. take the problem to the head of the organization
   C. take the problem to the person who gave him the assignment
   D. say nothing to anyone about his complaint

In answering this question, you should study each of the choices to find which is best. Consider choice "A" – Certainly an employee may discuss his complaint with fellow employees, but no change or improvement can result, and the complaint remains unresolved. Choice "B" is a poor choice since the head of the organization probably does not know what assignment you have been given, and taking your problem to him is known as "going over the head" of the supervisor. The supervisor, or person who made the assignment, is the person who can clarify it or correct any injustice. Choice "C" is, therefore, correct. To say nothing, as in choice "D," is unwise. Supervisors have and interest in knowing the problems employees are facing, and the employee is seeking a solution to his problem.

2) True/False Questions

The "true/false" or "right/wrong" form of question is sometimes used. Here a complete statement is given. Your job is to decide whether the statement is right or wrong.

SAMPLE: A roaming cell-phone call to a nearby city costs less than a non-roaming call to a distant city.

This statement is wrong, or false, since roaming calls are more expensive.
This is not a complete list of all possible question forms, although most of the others are variations of these common types. You will always get complete directions for

answering questions. Be sure you understand *how* to mark your answers – ask questions until you do.

V. RECORDING YOUR ANSWERS

Computer terminals are used more and more today for many different kinds of exams.

For an examination with very few applicants, you may be told to record your answers in the test booklet itself. Separate answer sheets are much more common. If this separate answer sheet is to be scored by machine – and this is often the case – it is highly important that you mark your answers correctly in order to get credit.

An electronic scoring machine is often used in civil service offices because of the speed with which papers can be scored. Machine-scored answer sheets must be marked with a pencil, which will be given to you. This pencil has a high graphite content which responds to the electronic scoring machine. As a matter of fact, stray dots may register as answers, so do not let your pencil rest on the answer sheet while you are pondering the correct answer. Also, if your pencil lead breaks or is otherwise defective, ask for another.

Since the answer sheet will be dropped in a slot in the scoring machine, be careful not to bend the corners or get the paper crumpled.

The answer sheet normally has five vertical columns of numbers, with 30 numbers to a column. These numbers correspond to the question numbers in your test booklet. After each number, going across the page are four or five pairs of dotted lines. These short dotted lines have small letters or numbers above them. The first two pairs may also have a "T" or "F" above the letters. This indicates that the first two pairs only are to be used if the questions are of the true-false type. If the questions are multiple choice, disregard the "T" and "F" and pay attention only to the small letters or numbers.

Answer your questions in the manner of the sample that follows:

32. The largest city in the United States is
    A. Washington, D.C.
    B. New York City
    C. Chicago
    D. Detroit
    E. San Francisco

1) Choose the answer you think is best. (New York City is the largest, so "B" is correct.)
2) Find the row of dotted lines numbered the same as the question you are answering. (Find row number 32)
3) Find the pair of dotted lines corresponding to the answer. (Find the pair of lines under the mark "B.")
4) Make a solid black mark between the dotted lines.

VI. BEFORE THE TEST

Common sense will help you find procedures to follow to get ready for an examination. Too many of us, however, overlook these sensible measures. Indeed, nervousness and fatigue have been found to be the most serious reasons why applicants fail to do their best on civil service tests. Here is a list of reminders:

- Begin your preparation early – Don't wait until the last minute to go scurrying around for books and materials or to find out what the position is all about.
- Prepare continuously – An hour a night for a week is better than an all-night cram session. This has been definitely established. What is more, a night a week for a month will return better dividends than crowding your study into a shorter period of time.
- Locate the place of the exam – You have been sent a notice telling you when and where to report for the examination. If the location is in a different town or otherwise unfamiliar to you, it would be well to inquire the best route and learn something about the building.
- Relax the night before the test – Allow your mind to rest. Do not study at all that night. Plan some mild recreation or diversion; then go to bed early and get a good night's sleep.
- Get up early enough to make a leisurely trip to the place for the test – This way unforeseen events, traffic snarls, unfamiliar buildings, etc. will not upset you.
- Dress comfortably – A written test is not a fashion show. You will be known by number and not by name, so wear something comfortable.
- Leave excess paraphernalia at home – Shopping bags and odd bundles will get in your way. You need bring only the items mentioned in the official notice you received; usually everything you need is provided. Do not bring reference books to the exam. They will only confuse those last minutes and be taken away from you when in the test room.
- Arrive somewhat ahead of time – If because of transportation schedules you must get there very early, bring a newspaper or magazine to take your mind off yourself while waiting.
- Locate the examination room – When you have found the proper room, you will be directed to the seat or part of the room where you will sit. Sometimes you are given a sheet of instructions to read while you are waiting. Do not fill out any forms until you are told to do so; just read them and be prepared.
- Relax and prepare to listen to the instructions
- If you have any physical problem that may keep you from doing your best, be sure to tell the test administrator. If you are sick or in poor health, you really cannot do your best on the exam. You can come back and take the test some other time.

VII. AT THE TEST

The day of the test is here and you have the test booklet in your hand. The temptation to get going is very strong. Caution! There is more to success than knowing the right answers. You must know how to identify your papers and understand variations in the type of short-answer question used in this particular examination. Follow these suggestions for maximum results from your efforts:

1) Cooperate with the monitor

The test administrator has a duty to create a situation in which you can be as much at ease as possible. He will give instructions, tell you when to begin, check to see that you are marking your answer sheet correctly, and so on. He is not there to guard you, although he will see that your competitors do not take unfair advantage. He wants to help you do your best.

2) Listen to all instructions

Don't jump the gun! Wait until you understand all directions. In most civil service tests you get more time than you need to answer the questions. So don't be in a hurry. Read each word of instructions until you clearly understand the meaning. Study the examples, listen to all announcements and follow directions. Ask questions if you do not understand what to do.

3) Identify your papers

Civil service exams are usually identified by number only. You will be assigned a number; you must not put your name on your test papers. Be sure to copy your number correctly. Since more than one exam may be given, copy your exact examination title.

4) Plan your time

Unless you are told that a test is a "speed" or "rate of work" test, speed itself is usually not important. Time enough to answer all the questions will be provided, but this does not mean that you have all day. An overall time limit has been set. Divide the total time (in minutes) by the number of questions to determine the approximate time you have for each question.

5) Do not linger over difficult questions

If you come across a difficult question, mark it with a paper clip (useful to have along) and come back to it when you have been through the booklet. One caution if you do this – be sure to skip a number on your answer sheet as well. Check often to be sure that you have not lost your place and that you are marking in the row numbered the same as the question you are answering.

6) Read the questions

Be sure you know what the question asks! Many capable people are unsuccessful because they failed to *read* the questions correctly.

7) Answer all questions

Unless you have been instructed that a penalty will be deducted for incorrect answers, it is better to guess than to omit a question.

8) Speed tests

It is often better NOT to guess on speed tests. It has been found that on timed tests people are tempted to spend the last few seconds before time is called in marking answers at random – without even reading them – in the hope of picking up a few extra points. To discourage this practice, the instructions may warn you that your score will be "corrected" for guessing. That is, a penalty will be applied. The incorrect answers will be deducted from the correct ones, or some other penalty formula will be used.

9) Review your answers

If you finish before time is called, go back to the questions you guessed or omitted to give them further thought. Review other answers if you have time.

10) Return your test materials

If you are ready to leave before others have finished or time is called, take ALL your materials to the monitor and leave quietly. Never take any test material with you. The monitor can discover whose papers are not complete, and taking a test booklet may be grounds for disqualification.

VIII. EXAMINATION TECHNIQUES

1) Read the general instructions carefully. These are usually printed on the first page of the exam booklet. As a rule, these instructions refer to the timing of the examination; the fact that you should not start work until the signal and must stop work at a signal, etc. If there are any *special* instructions, such as a choice of questions to be answered, make sure that you note this instruction carefully.

2) When you are ready to start work on the examination, that is as soon as the signal has been given, read the instructions to each question booklet, underline any key words or phrases, such as *least, best, outline, describe* and the like. In this way you will tend to answer as requested rather than discover on reviewing your paper that you *listed without describing*, that you selected the *worst* choice rather than the *best* choice, etc.

3) If the examination is of the objective or multiple-choice type – that is, each question will also give a series of possible answers: A, B, C or D, and you are called upon to select the best answer and write the letter next to that answer on your answer paper – it is advisable to start answering each question in turn. There may be anywhere from 50 to 100 such questions in the three or four hours allotted and you can see how much time would be taken if you read through all the questions before beginning to answer any. Furthermore, if you come across a question or group of questions which you know would be difficult to answer, it would undoubtedly affect your handling of all the other questions.

4) If the examination is of the essay type and contains but a few questions, it is a moot point as to whether you should read all the questions before starting to answer any one. Of course, if you are given a choice – say five out of seven and the like – then it is essential to read all the questions so you can eliminate the two that are most difficult. If, however, you are asked to answer all the questions, there may be danger in trying to answer the easiest one first because you may find that you will spend too much time on it. The best technique is to answer the first question, then proceed to the second, etc.

5) Time your answers. Before the exam begins, write down the time it started, then add the time allowed for the examination and write down the time it must be completed, then divide the time available somewhat as follows:

- If 3-1/2 hours are allowed, that would be 210 minutes. If you have 80 objective-type questions, that would be an average of 2-1/2 minutes per question. Allow yourself no more than 2 minutes per question, or a total of 160 minutes, which will permit about 50 minutes to review.
- If for the time allotment of 210 minutes there are 7 essay questions to answer, that would average about 30 minutes a question. Give yourself only 25 minutes per question so that you have about 35 minutes to review.

6) The most important instruction is to *read each question* and make sure you know what is wanted. The second most important instruction is to *time yourself properly* so that you answer every question. The third most important instruction is to *answer every question*. Guess if you have to but include something for each question. Remember that you will receive no credit for a blank and will probably receive some credit if you write something in answer to an essay question. If you guess a letter – say "B" for a multiple-choice question – you may have guessed right. If you leave a blank as an answer to a multiple-choice question, the examiners may respect your feelings but it will not add a point to your score. Some exams may penalize you for wrong answers, so in such cases *only*, you may not want to guess unless you have some basis for your answer.

7) Suggestions
   a. Objective-type questions
      1. Examine the question booklet for proper sequence of pages and questions
      2. Read all instructions carefully
      3. Skip any question which seems too difficult; return to it after all other questions have been answered
      4. Apportion your time properly; do not spend too much time on any single question or group of questions
      5. Note and underline key words – *all, most, fewest, least, best, worst, same, opposite,* etc.
      6. Pay particular attention to negatives
      7. Note unusual option, e.g., unduly long, short, complex, different or similar in content to the body of the question
      8. Observe the use of "hedging" words – *probably, may, most likely,* etc.
      9. Make sure that your answer is put next to the same number as the question
      10. Do not second-guess unless you have good reason to believe the second answer is definitely more correct
      11. Cross out original answer if you decide another answer is more accurate; do not erase until you are ready to hand your paper in
      12. Answer all questions; guess unless instructed otherwise
      13. Leave time for review

   b. Essay questions
      1. Read each question carefully
      2. Determine exactly what is wanted. Underline key words or phrases.
      3. Decide on outline or paragraph answer

4. Include many different points and elements unless asked to develop any one or two points or elements
5. Show impartiality by giving pros and cons unless directed to select one side only
6. Make and write down any assumptions you find necessary to answer the questions
7. Watch your English, grammar, punctuation and choice of words
8. Time your answers; don't crowd material

8) Answering the essay question

Most essay questions can be answered by framing the specific response around several key words or ideas. Here are a few such key words or ideas:

M's: manpower, materials, methods, money, management
P's: purpose, program, policy, plan, procedure, practice, problems, pitfalls, personnel, public relations
   a. Six basic steps in handling problems:
      1. Preliminary plan and background development
      2. Collect information, data and facts
      3. Analyze and interpret information, data and facts
      4. Analyze and develop solutions as well as make recommendations
      5. Prepare report and sell recommendations
      6. Install recommendations and follow up effectiveness

   b. Pitfalls to avoid
      1. *Taking things for granted* – A statement of the situation does not necessarily imply that each of the elements is necessarily true; for example, a complaint may be invalid and biased so that all that can be taken for granted is that a complaint has been registered
      2. *Considering only one side of a situation* – Wherever possible, indicate several alternatives and then point out the reasons you selected the best one
      3. *Failing to indicate follow up* – Whenever your answer indicates action on your part, make certain that you will take proper follow-up action to see how successful your recommendations, procedures or actions turn out to be
      4. *Taking too long in answering any single question* – Remember to time your answers properly

IX. AFTER THE TEST

Scoring procedures differ in detail among civil service jurisdictions although the general principles are the same. Whether the papers are hand-scored or graded by machine we have described, they are nearly always graded by number. That is, the person who marks the paper knows only the number – never the name – of the applicant. Not until all the papers have been graded will they be matched with names. If other tests, such as training and experience or oral interview ratings have been given, scores will be combined. Different parts of the examination usually have different weights. For example, the written test might count 60 percent of the final grade, and a rating of training and experience 40 percent. In many jurisdictions, veterans will have a certain number of points added to their grades.

After the final grade has been determined, the names are placed in grade order and an eligible list is established. There are various methods for resolving ties between those who get the same final grade – probably the most common is to place first the name of the person whose application was received first. Job offers are made from the eligible list in the order the names appear on it. You will be notified of your grade and your rank as soon as all these computations have been made. This will be done as rapidly as possible.

People who are found to meet the requirements in the announcement are called "eligibles." Their names are put on a list of eligible candidates. An eligible's chances of getting a job depend on how high he stands on this list and how fast agencies are filling jobs from the list.

When a job is to be filled from a list of eligibles, the agency asks for the names of people on the list of eligibles for that job. When the civil service commission receives this request, it sends to the agency the names of the three people highest on this list. Or, if the job to be filled has specialized requirements, the office sends the agency the names of the top three persons who meet these requirements from the general list.

The appointing officer makes a choice from among the three people whose names were sent to him. If the selected person accepts the appointment, the names of the others are put back on the list to be considered for future openings.

That is the rule in hiring from all kinds of eligible lists, whether they are for typist, carpenter, chemist, or something else. For every vacancy, the appointing officer has his choice of any one of the top three eligibles on the list. This explains why the person whose name is on top of the list sometimes does not get an appointment when some of the persons lower on the list do. If the appointing officer chooses the second or third eligible, the No. 1 eligible does not get a job at once, but stays on the list until he is appointed or the list is terminated.

X. HOW TO PASS THE INTERVIEW TEST

The examination for which you applied requires an oral interview test. You have already taken the written test and you are now being called for the interview test – the final part of the formal examination.

You may think that it is not possible to prepare for an interview test and that there are no procedures to follow during an interview. Our purpose is to point out some things you can do in advance that will help you and some good rules to follow and pitfalls to avoid while you are being interviewed.

What is an interview supposed to test?
The written examination is designed to test the technical knowledge and competence of the candidate; the oral is designed to evaluate intangible qualities, not readily measured otherwise, and to establish a list showing the relative fitness of each candidate – as measured against his competitors – for the position sought. Scoring is not on the basis of "right" and "wrong," but on a sliding scale of values ranging from "not passable" to "outstanding." As a matter of fact, it is possible to achieve a relatively low score without a single "incorrect" answer because of evident weakness in the qualities being measured.

Occasionally, an examination may consist entirely of an oral test – either an individual or a group oral. In such cases, information is sought concerning the technical knowledges and abilities of the candidate, since there has been no written examination for this purpose. More commonly, however, an oral test is used to supplement a written examination.

Who conducts interviews?

The composition of oral boards varies among different jurisdictions. In nearly all, a representative of the personnel department serves as chairman. One of the members of the board may be a representative of the department in which the candidate would work. In some cases, "outside experts" are used, and, frequently, a businessman or some other representative of the general public is asked to serve. Labor and management or other special groups may be represented. The aim is to secure the services of experts in the appropriate field.

However the board is composed, it is a good idea (and not at all improper or unethical) to ascertain in advance of the interview who the members are and what groups they represent. When you are introduced to them, you will have some idea of their backgrounds and interests, and at least you will not stutter and stammer over their names.

What should be done before the interview?

While knowledge about the board members is useful and takes some of the surprise element out of the interview, there is other preparation which is more substantive. It *is* possible to prepare for an oral interview – in several ways:

1) Keep a copy of your application and review it carefully before the interview

This may be the only document before the oral board, and the starting point of the interview. Know what education and experience you have listed there, and the sequence and dates of all of it. Sometimes the board will ask you to review the highlights of your experience for them; you should not have to hem and haw doing it.

2) Study the class specification and the examination announcement

Usually, the oral board has one or both of these to guide them. The qualities, characteristics or knowledges required by the position sought are stated in these documents. They offer valuable clues as to the nature of the oral interview. For example, if the job involves supervisory responsibilities, the announcement will usually indicate that knowledge of modern supervisory methods and the qualifications of the candidate as a supervisor will be tested. If so, you can expect such questions, frequently in the form of a hypothetical situation which you are expected to solve. NEVER go into an oral without knowledge of the duties and responsibilities of the job you seek.

3) Think through each qualification required

Try to visualize the kind of questions you would ask if you were a board member. How well could you answer them? Try especially to appraise your own knowledge and background in each area, *measured against the job sought*, and identify any areas in which you are weak. Be critical and realistic – do not flatter yourself.

4) Do some general reading in areas in which you feel you may be weak

For example, if the job involves supervision and your past experience has NOT, some general reading in supervisory methods and practices, particularly in the field of human relations, might be useful. Do NOT study agency procedures or detailed manuals. The oral board will be testing your understanding and capacity, not your memory.

5) Get a good night's sleep and watch your general health and mental attitude

You will want a clear head at the interview. Take care of a cold or any other minor ailment, and of course, no hangovers.

What should be done on the day of the interview?

Now comes the day of the interview itself. Give yourself plenty of time to get there. Plan to arrive somewhat ahead of the scheduled time, particularly if your appointment is in the fore part of the day. If a previous candidate fails to appear, the board might be ready for you a bit early. By early afternoon an oral board is almost invariably behind schedule if there are many candidates, and you may have to wait. Take along a book or magazine to read, or your application to review, but leave any extraneous material in the waiting room when you go in for your interview. In any event, relax and compose yourself.

The matter of dress is important. The board is forming impressions about you – from your experience, your manners, your attitude, and your appearance. Give your personal appearance careful attention. Dress your best, but not your flashiest. Choose conservative, appropriate clothing, and be sure it is immaculate. This is a business interview, and your appearance should indicate that you regard it as such. Besides, being well groomed and properly dressed will help boost your confidence.

Sooner or later, someone will call your name and escort you into the interview room. *This is it.* From here on you are on your own. It is too late for any more preparation. But remember, you asked for this opportunity to prove your fitness, and you are here because your request was granted.

What happens when you go in?

The usual sequence of events will be as follows: The clerk (who is often the board stenographer) will introduce you to the chairman of the oral board, who will introduce you to the other members of the board. Acknowledge the introductions before you sit down. Do not be surprised if you find a microphone facing you or a stenotypist sitting by. Oral interviews are usually recorded in the event of an appeal or other review.

Usually the chairman of the board will open the interview by reviewing the highlights of your education and work experience from your application – primarily for the benefit of the other members of the board, as well as to get the material into the record. Do not interrupt or comment unless there is an error or significant misinterpretation; if that is the case, do not hesitate. But do not quibble about insignificant matters. Also, he will usually ask you some question about your education, experience or your present job – partly to get you to start talking and to establish the interviewing "rapport." He may start the actual questioning, or turn it over to one of the other members. Frequently, each member undertakes the questioning on a particular area, one in which he is perhaps most competent, so you can expect each member to participate in the examination. Because time is limited, you may also expect some rather abrupt switches in the direction the questioning takes, so do not be upset by it. Normally, a board member will not pursue a single line of questioning unless he discovers a particular strength or weakness.

After each member has participated, the chairman will usually ask whether any member has any further questions, then will ask you if you have anything you wish to add. Unless you are expecting this question, it may floor you. Worse, it may start you off on an extended, extemporaneous speech. The board is not usually seeking more information. The question is principally to offer you a last opportunity to present further qualifications or to indicate that you have nothing to add. So, if you feel that a significant qualification or characteristic has been overlooked, it is proper to point it out in a sentence or so. Do not compliment the board on the thoroughness of their examination – they have been sketchy, and you know it. If you wish, merely say, "No thank you, I have nothing further to add." This is a point where you can "talk yourself out" of a good impression or fail to present an important bit of information. Remember, *you close the interview yourself.*

The chairman will then say, "That is all, Mr. _____, thank you." Do not be startled; the interview is over, and quicker than you think. Thank him, gather your belongings and take your leave. Save your sigh of relief for the other side of the door.

How to put your best foot forward

Throughout this entire process, you may feel that the board individually and collectively is trying to pierce your defenses, seek out your hidden weaknesses and embarrass and confuse you. Actually, this is not true. They are obliged to make an appraisal of your qualifications for the job you are seeking, and they want to see you in your best light. Remember, they must interview all candidates and a non-cooperative candidate may become a failure in spite of their best efforts to bring out his qualifications. Here are 15 suggestions that will help you:

1) Be natural – Keep your attitude confident, not cocky

If you are not confident that you can do the job, do not expect the board to be. Do not apologize for your weaknesses, try to bring out your strong points. The board is interested in a positive, not negative, presentation. Cockiness will antagonize any board member and make him wonder if you are covering up a weakness by a false show of strength.

2) Get comfortable, but don't lounge or sprawl

Sit erectly but not stiffly. A careless posture may lead the board to conclude that you are careless in other things, or at least that you are not impressed by the importance of the occasion. Either conclusion is natural, even if incorrect. Do not fuss with your clothing, a pencil or an ashtray. Your hands may occasionally be useful to emphasize a point; do not let them become a point of distraction.

3) Do not wisecrack or make small talk

This is a serious situation, and your attitude should show that you consider it as such. Further, the time of the board is limited – they do not want to waste it, and neither should you.

4) Do not exaggerate your experience or abilities

In the first place, from information in the application or other interviews and sources, the board may know more about you than you think. Secondly, you probably will not get away with it. An experienced board is rather adept at spotting such a situation, so do not take the chance.

5) If you know a board member, do not make a point of it, yet do not hide it
Certainly you are not fooling him, and probably not the other members of the board. Do not try to take advantage of your acquaintanceship – it will probably do you little good.

6) Do not dominate the interview
Let the board do that. They will give you the clues – do not assume that you have to do all the talking. Realize that the board has a number of questions to ask you, and do not try to take up all the interview time by showing off your extensive knowledge of the answer to the first one.

7) Be attentive
You only have 20 minutes or so, and you should keep your attention at its sharpest throughout. When a member is addressing a problem or question to you, give him your undivided attention. Address your reply principally to him, but do not exclude the other board members.

8) Do not interrupt
A board member may be stating a problem for you to analyze. He will ask you a question when the time comes. Let him state the problem, and wait for the question.

9) Make sure you understand the question
Do not try to answer until you are sure what the question is. If it is not clear, restate it in your own words or ask the board member to clarify it for you. However, do not haggle about minor elements.

10) Reply promptly but not hastily
A common entry on oral board rating sheets is "candidate responded readily," or "candidate hesitated in replies." Respond as promptly and quickly as you can, but do not jump to a hasty, ill-considered answer.

11) Do not be peremptory in your answers
A brief answer is proper – but do not fire your answer back. That is a losing game from your point of view. The board member can probably ask questions much faster than you can answer them.

12) Do not try to create the answer you think the board member wants
He is interested in what kind of mind you have and how it works – not in playing games. Furthermore, he can usually spot this practice and will actually grade you down on it.

13) Do not switch sides in your reply merely to agree with a board member
Frequently, a member will take a contrary position merely to draw you out and to see if you are willing and able to defend your point of view. Do not start a debate, yet do not surrender a good position. If a position is worth taking, it is worth defending.

14) Do not be afraid to admit an error in judgment if you are shown to be wrong

The board knows that you are forced to reply without any opportunity for careful consideration. Your answer may be demonstrably wrong. If so, admit it and get on with the interview.

15) Do not dwell at length on your present job

The opening question may relate to your present assignment. Answer the question but do not go into an extended discussion. You are being examined for a *new* job, not your present one. As a matter of fact, try to phrase ALL your answers in terms of the job for which you are being examined.

Basis of Rating

Probably you will forget most of these "do's" and "don'ts" when you walk into the oral interview room. Even remembering them all will not ensure you a passing grade. Perhaps you did not have the qualifications in the first place. But remembering them will help you to put your best foot forward, without treading on the toes of the board members.

Rumor and popular opinion to the contrary notwithstanding, an oral board wants you to make the best appearance possible. They know you are under pressure – but they also want to see how you respond to it as a guide to what your reaction would be under the pressures of the job you seek. They will be influenced by the degree of poise you display, the personal traits you show and the manner in which you respond.

ABOUT THIS BOOK

This book contains tests divided into Examination Sections. Go through each test, answering every question in the margin. At the end of each test look at the answer key and check your answers. On the ones you got wrong, look at the right answer choice and learn. Do not fill in the answers first. Do not memorize the questions and answers, but understand the answer and principles involved. On your test, the questions will likely be different from the samples. Questions are changed and new ones added. If you understand these past questions you should have success with any changes that arise. Tests may consist of several types of questions. We have additional books on each subject should more study be advisable or necessary for you. Finally, the more you study, the better prepared you will be. This book is intended to be the last thing you study before you walk into the examination room. Prior study of relevant texts is also recommended. NLC publishes some of these in our Fundamental Series. Knowledge and good sense are important factors in passing your exam. Good luck also helps. So now study this Passbook, absorb the material contained within and take that knowledge into the examination. Then do your best to pass that exam.

EXAMINATION SECTION

EXAMINATION SECTION
TEST 1

DIRECTIONS: Each question or incomplete statement is followed by several suggested answers or completions. Select the one that BEST answers the question or completes the statement. *PRINT THE LETTER OF THE CORRECT ANSWER IN THE SPACE AT THE RIGHT.*

1. Which one of the following are concerns of a data entry operator?
   A. Usage of abbreviations
   B. Glossary
   C. Working dictionary
   D. All of the above

   1.____

2. Which one of the following is important to keep unique information in the file?
   A. Identification numbers
   B. Tables
   C. Records
   D. All of the above

   2.____

3. Identification numbers are mostly concerned with
   A. sample ID
   B. original station
   C. none of the above
   D. both A and B

   3.____

4. Which one of the following could be entered into a data table?
   A. Test data
   B. Testing label
   C. Replicate number
   D. All of the above

   4.____

5. Measured data values are intended to place in
   A. empty fields
   B. concentration field
   C. both A and B
   D. none of the above

   5.____

6. Any note or comment could be added to
   A. qualifier column
   B. first column
   C. none of the above
   D. both A and B

   6.____

7. Information processing emphasizes
   A. tabulating
   B. auditing
   C. verifying
   D. all of the above

   7.____

8. Analysis of data is based on
   A. principals
   B. reasons
   C. data division
   D. all of the above

   8.____

9. Which one of the following is NOT included in a data entry operator's responsibilities?
   A. Device usage
   B. Technical knowledge
   C. Character and discretion
   D. All of the above

   9.____

10. Document scanning could be done through   10.____
   - A. OCR
   - B. OMR
   - C. both A and B
   - D. none of the above

11. _____ are used to fill out empty fields in scanned images of data.   11.____
   - A. Computerized optical scanners
   - B. OCR software
   - C. Scanners
   - D. All of the above

12. Personal records, sensitive information, and financial information is checked by a   12.____
   - A. data entry clerk
   - B. machine
   - C. both A and B
   - D. none of the above

13. Pre-processes is a technique used by _____ to improve recognition.   13.____
   - A. OCR
   - B. OMR
   - C. none of the above
   - D. both A and B

14. Handwritten data is captured through   14.____
   - A. OMR
   - B. ICR
   - C. OCR
   - D. none of the above

15. Meaningful information is an important concern of   15.____
   - A. data entry
   - B. data processing
   - C. data retrieval
   - D. all of the above

16. Which one of the following is a data analysis software?   16.____
   - A. SAS
   - B. SPSS
   - C. DAP
   - D. All of the above

17. Electronic data processing is more beneficial for   17.____
   - A. commercial data
   - B. scientific data
   - C. mathematical data
   - D. all of the above

18. Repetition of data is checked through   18.____
   - A. integrity checks
   - B. validation
   - C. verification
   - D. both A and B

19. Entered data must be   19.____
   - A. clean
   - B. complete
   - C. useful
   - D. all of the above

20. Which one of the following is NOT a characteristic of a data dictionary?   20.____
   - A. Data name
   - B. Origin
   - C. Destination
   - D. None of the above

21. Which one of the following is NOT a DDL (data definition language) command?   21.____
   - A. Create table
   - B. Drop table
   - C. Alter table
   - D. None of the above

22. _____ mains data in tables.
    A. Transactions   B. Metadata
    C. Commit statement   D. All of the above

                                                        22._____

23. Data dictionary is another name for
    A. metadata   B. table
    C. record   D. both A and B

                                                         23._____

24. Length, limits, and remarks are concerns of
    A. data elements   B. transactions
    C. metadata   D. both A and B

                                                      24._____

25. Data entry could be
    A. online   B. offline
    C. none of the above   D. both A and B

                                                   25._____

KEY (CORRECT ANSWERS)

1.	D		11.	A
2.	A		12.	C
3.	D		13.	A
4.	D		14.	A
5.	B		15.	D
6.	A		16.	D
7.	D		17.	A
8.	D		18.	A
9.	B		19.	D
10.	C		20.	D

21.	D
22.	A
23.	A
24.	A
25.	A

TEST 2

1. Data entry into a computerized database could be done by an individual, as well as by a
   A. machine
   B. software
   C. both A and B
   D. none of the above

   1.____

2. Which one of the following is a data entry machine?
   A. Keyboard
   B. Optical scanner
   C. Data recorder
   D. All of the above

   2.____

3. Electronic data processing is done by
   A. optical character recognition
   B. optical mark recognition
   C. both A and B
   D. none of the above

   3.____

4. Accuracy of electronic data processing depends on the
   A. original document
   B. scanned image
   C. experience of the person
   D. all of the above

   4.____

5. Data processing is a subclass of _____ processing.
   A. knowledge
   B. information
   C. both A and B
   D. none of the above

   5.____

6. Which one of the following is NOT a data processing function?
   A. Sorting
   B. Aggregation
   C. Reporting
   D. None of the above

   6.____

7. Few computational operations are involved in _____ data processing.
   A. commercial
   B. real estate
   C. both A and B
   D. none of the above

   7.____

8. Which one of the following is a data processing system by application?
   A. Scientific data processing system
   B. Transaction processing system
   C. Process control system
   D. All of the above

   8.____

9. Check register is an example of
   A. data processing
   B. information retrieval
   C. both A and B
   D. none of the above

   9.____

10. Poor form design and human errors occur MOSTLY in
    A. online data entry
    B. offline data entry
    C. both A and B
    D. none of the above

    10.____

11. Errors in data entry could be reduced by implementing which strategy?   11.____
    A. Good form design   B. Reducing key strokes
    C. Error feedback   D. All of the above

12. Forms batched is an error which occurs in   12.____
    A. offline data entry   B. online data entry
    C. both A and B   D. none of the above

13. Which one of the following is an interactive data input method?   13.____
    A, Menus   B. Templates
    C. Commands   D. All of the above

14. Unique codes used in data entry help in   14.____
    A. cross reference   B. efficient storage
    C. easy access   D. all of the above

15. Validation checks are applied when _____ data is input.   15.____
    A. large   B. commercial
    C. numeric   D. all of the above

16. What is TRUE for stored procedure?   16.____
    A. Mini program   B. Executable code
    C. None of the above   D. Both A and B

17. _____ checks values by adding them individually.   17.____
    A. Stored procedures   B. Record totals
    C. Batch control   D. All of the above

18. Data quality is concerned with   18.____
    A. standard   B. excellence
    C. completeness   D. all of the above

19. _____ is the process of correcting data to USA and worldwide4 postal   19.____
    standards.
    A. Data proofing   B. Geocoding
    C. Both A and B   D. None of the above

20. Profiling of the data tracks _____ in data.   20.____
    A. anomalies   B. inconsistencies
    C. both A and B   D. none of the above

21. Which one is NOT a part of the data quality control process?   21.____
    A. Severity   B. Precision
    C. Both A and B   D. None of the above

22. Which one of the following is a data validation process?   22.____
    A. Data type validation   B. Range and constraint validation
    C. Structured validation   D. All of the above

23. Which validation method checks for missing records?
   A. Batch totals
   B. Consistency checks
   C. Control totals
   D. All of the above

23.____

24. Numeric data validation is done through
   A. hash totals
   B. check digits
   C. data type checks
   D. both A and B

24.____

25. _____ tracks that important data is not being missed.
   A. Data type check
   B. Limit check
   C. Presence check
   D. All of the above

25.____

KEY (CORRECT ANSWERS)

1.	A		11.	D
2.	D		12.	B
3.	C		13.	D
4.	D		14.	D
5.	B		15.	A
6.	D		16.	D
7.	A		17.	B
8.	A		18.	D
9.	A		19.	B
10.	B		20.	C

21.	C
22.	D
23.	A
24.	B
25.	C

TEST 3

DIRECTIONS: Each question or incomplete statement is followed by several suggested answers or completions. Select the one that BEST answers the question or completes the statement. *PRINT THE LETTER OF THE CORRECT ANSWER IN THE SPACE AT THE RIGHT.*

1. Automated data collection captures data from   1.____
    A. handwritten documents   B. forms
    C. coupons   D. all of the above

2. _____ collects information from electronic resources as well as from   2.____
manual papers.
    A. Document imaging   B. OCR
    C. Both A and B   D. None of the above

3. Which of the following is a cost effective solution for data capture?   3.____
    A. Document scanning   B. OMR
    C. OCR   D. Both A and C

4. Which data entry software deals with machine prints?   4.____
    A. OCR   B. OMR
    C. ICR   D. None of the above

5. Handwritten documents are captured through   5.____
    A. ICR   B. scanner
    C. OMR   D. all of the above

6. _____ collects numerous pieces of data.   6.____
    A. Reporting   B. Aggregation
    C. Both A and B   D. Classification

7. Items are arranged in some order by applying   7.____
    A. analysis   B. classifying
    C. sorting   D. all of the above

8. When a user enters a query into the system, which one of the following   8.___
processes starts?
    A. Information retrieval   B. Data processing
    C. Electronic data processing   D. All of the above

9. Which of the following data entry software?   9.___
    A. Entry point i4   B. Contact zone
    C. Capturx   D. All of the above

10. Usually _____ is the best choice to scan invoices and forms.   10.____
    A. OMR   B. ICR
    C. Scanner   D. all of the above

11. Duplication of rows breaks _____ rules.   11._____
    A. consistency   B. integrity
    C. accuracy   D. all of the above

12. Which one of the following is NOT a recording method for magnetic tape?   12._____
    A. Linear   B. Scanning
    C. Both A and B   D. None of the above

13. Sequence numbering detects _____ in large data input.   13._____
    A. missing records   B. invalid
    C. valid   D. all of the above

14. Which one of the following is used to detect errors in the data?   14._____
    A. Controlled redundancy   B. Control digits
    C. Both A and B   D. None of the above

15. Inter-field relationship check is applicable only for _____ fields.   15._____
    A. individual   B. valid
    C. invalid   D. none of the above

16. If there are multiple categories to be entered, then a _____ is assigned   16._____
to each category.
    A. block number   B. identifier
    C. number   D. all of the above

17. Which one of the following is NOT true for significant codes?   17._____
    A. Meaningful   B. Expandable
    C. Concise   D. All of the above

18. A large set of data input is coded. Which of the following is TRUE for   18._____
coding scheme?
    A. Concise   B. Precise
    C. Comprehensive   D. All of the above

19. Which types of errors are tracked in individual data fields?   19._____
    A. Inconsistent data   B. Missing data
    C. Incorrect data   D. All of the above

20. Verification is applied on large data for _____ input.   20._____
    A. single   B. dual
    C. multiple   D. all of the above

21. Data quality strategy of an organization must be   21._____
    A. defined   B. well implemented
    C. clear   D. all of the above

22. Data scrubbing is another name for   22._____
    A. data cleansing   B. data cleaning
    C. both A and B   D. none of the above

23. Typographical errors are removed during   23.____
    A. data integrity   B. data cleansing
    C. data consistency   D. none of the above

24. _____ handles complex data processing.   24.____
    A. Structured validation   B. Data type validation
    C. Cross reference validation   D. Both A and B

25. A valid number of related records is recorded by   25.____
    A. cardinality check   B. batch totals
    C. control totals   D. all of the above

KEY (CORRECT ANSWERS)

1.	D		11.	B
2.	A		12.	D
3.	D		13.	A
4.	A		14.	C
5.	A		15.	A
6.	B		16.	A
7.	C		17.	C
8.	A		18.	D
9.	D		19.	D
10.	A		20.	B

21. D
22. C
23. B
24. A
25. A

9

TEST 4

DIRECTIONS: Each question or incomplete statement is followed by several suggested answers or completions. Select the one that BEST answers the question or completes the statement. *PRINT THE LETTER OF THE CORRECT ANSWER IN THE SPACE AT THE RIGHT.*

1. Recognition software can get information from
   A. email
   B. paper
   C. fax
   D. all of the above

   1.____

2. Which one of the following are vital fundamentals of ReadSoft's automatic data capture technology?
   A. OCR
   B. OMR
   C. ICR
   D. None of the above

   2.____

3. OCR scanning technology is concerned with
   A. images only
   B. text only
   C. any type of data
   D. none of the above

   3.____

4. Bar code recognition is a method of data
   A. processing
   B. capturing
   C. preserving
   D. both B and C

   4.____

5. CallXpres is used to capture
   A. invoice
   B. voice
   C. emails
   D. all of the above

   5.____

6. Which one of the following is NOT an automated input method for data collection?
   A. Touch sensitive screen
   B. MICR
   C. OMR
   D. All of the above

   6.____

7. Smart cards are also a method for data
   A. validation
   B. collection
   C. processing
   D. none of the above

   7.____

8. _____ use electronic forms to capture data from websites and then sent to the database.
   A. Web data capture
   B. OCR
   C. ICR
   D. All of the above

   8.____

9. _____ is BEST suitable in data entry and word processing environments.
   A. Voice recognition
   B. Bar code recognition
   C. ICR
   D. None of the above

   9.____

10. Which data collection method is BEST to confirm identity?
    A. Smart cards
    B. Magnetic stripe cards
    C. ID cards
    D. All of the above

    10.____

11. Feedback for all entries excluding _____ keeps integrity of data.
    A. confidential information   B. numeric data
    C. prices   D. all of the above
11.____

12. Which is TRUE for error-free data entry?
    A. Fast response   B. Single method
    C. Specific display   D. All of the above
12.____

13. A consistent method of data change includes
    A. insert   B. delete
    C. both A and B   D. none of the above
13.____

14. Short length data items are helpful in _____ data entry.
    A. numeric   B. alphabets
    C. alphanumeric   D. both A and C
14.____

15. If long data items must be entered, what will be the BEST approach?
    A. Partitioning   B. Coding
    C. Use of symbols   D. Both A and C
15.____

16. Distinctive abbreviations are used to _____ data input.
    A. recognize   B. shorten
    C. display   D. all of the above
16.____

17. Upper and lower case entries must be equivalent if data is
    A. coded   B. duplicate
    C. large   D. none of the above
17.____

18. Single and multiple blank characters are considered _____ in data input.
    A. equivalent   B. different
    C. a bit different   D. none of the above
18.____

19. Which one of the following is essential for graphic data entry?
    A. Plotting symbol   B. Line type
    C. Text font   D. All of the above
19.____

20. Which display attribute could be changed in graphic data?
    A. Color   B. Line type
    C. Cross-hatching   D. All of the above
20.____

21. Scaling and graph construction are concerned with _____ input.
    A. graphic   B. numeric
    C. large   D. none of the above
21.____

22. Repetitive data entry must be checked before starting another
    A. operation   B. transaction
    C. none of the above   D. both A and B
22.____

23. Which one is NOT true for data processing?   23._____
    A. Default values   B. Defaults for sequential entries
    C. Default values display   D. None of the above

24. Simple data fields are validated by   24._____
    A. structured validation   B. data type validation
    C. range and constraint validation D. both A and B

25. Simple rang and constraint validation is used to validate the sequence of   25._____
    A. rows   B. tables
    C. characters   D. none of the above

———————

KEY (CORRECT ANSWERS)

1.	D		11.	A
2.	A		12.	D
3.	C		13.	C
4.	B		14.	A
5.	A		15.	D
6.	A		16.	B
7.	B		17.	A
8.	A		18.	A
9.	A		19.	D
10.	B		20.	D

21.	D
22.	B
23.	A
24.	B
25.	D

———————

EXAMINATION SECTION
TEST 1

DIRECTIONS: Each question or incomplete statement is followed by several suggested answers or completions. Select the one that BEST answers the question or completes the statement. *PRINT THE LETTER OF THE CORRECT ANSWER IN THE SPACE AT THE RIGHT.*

1. The _____ on the data processing staff is responsible for determining if a new applica-   1._____
    tion should be developed.

    A. programmer   B. analyst
    C. operator   D. database administrator
    E. all of the above

2. A collection of files grouped together so that data may be independently retrieved from   2._____
    each file is a

    A. file   B. record
    C. database   D. file management system
    E. data bank

3. The data processing cycle consists of input,   3._____

    A. processing, output
    B. arithmetic, logic, output
    C. storage, output
    D. processing, storage, output
    E. arithmetic, logic, storage, output

4. Before any data may be processed, it MUST reside   4._____

    A. on tape   B. on video cards
    C. in computer memory   D. on the video screen
    E. on the printer

5. _____ may be stored on magnetic disk.   5._____

    A. Characters   B. Fields   C. Records
    D. Databases   E. All of the above

6. An example of a source document is a   6._____

    A. bill produced by a computer
    B. a graph generated by a spreadsheet program
    C. handwritten list of items to be entered into a computer
    D. checking statement sent by a bank to a customer
    E. all of the above

7. Data integrity refers to _____ entry of data into the computer system.   7._____

    A. accurate   B. reliable   C. timely
    D. all of the above   E. none of the above

8. The process of arranging a list of names in alphabetical order is called   8.___

    A. indexing   B. sorting   C. reporting
    D. searching   E. selection

9. The MAIN components of a computerized report are   9.___

    A. heading, detail lines, summary
    B. data entry screen, editing area, data validation area
    C. heading, control breaks, summary
    D. heading, subtotal lines, summary
    E. heading and summary lines

10. _____ terminals are computer terminals which also have processing capabilities.   10.___

    A. Keyboard   B. Dumb
    C. Remote job entry   D. Intelligent
    E. Stand-alone

11. The process of transferring data over a communication line from a mainframe computer   11.___
     to a microcomputer is

    A. uploading   B. downloading
    C. modem transmission   D. electronic mail
    E. networking

12. During _____, data is entered onto storage media, then re-entered again to ensure the 12.___
     accuracy of the data.

    A. editing   B. validation checking
    C. bi-keying   D. key verification
    E. double verification

13. A(n) _____ printer is an example of a high-speed printer.   13.___

    A. ink jet   B. laser   C. thermal
    D. photo   E. all of the above

14. A(n) _____ report is NOT produced by a computer.   14.___

    A. detail   B. exception   C. projection
    D. summary   E. all of the above

15. A _____ video screen displays only one color.   15.___

    A. VGA   B. color   C. monochrome
    D. CRT   E. all of the above

16. The _____ printer is BEST suited to print graphic output.   16.___

    A. dot matrix   B. ink jet   C. plotter
    D. chain   E. thermal

17. Which of the following can be used for entering data into a computer?   17.___

    A. OCR   B. Mouse   C. Keyboard
    D. Light pen   E. All of the above

18. Database management systems use a special class of commands in order that a user may facilitate extracting data from the database.
This class of commands is called _____ language.

18.____

    A. query by example   B. query
    C. inquiry   D. programming
    E. procedure

19. An acceptable response time from when the user requests data from the computer to the time the user receives a response is under _____ seconds.

19.____

    A. 60   B. 30   C. 15   D. 10   E. 3

20. The part of computer memory which may be accessed by the user for storage and retrieving his own data is called

20.____

    A. RAM   B. ROM   C. EPROM   D. PROM   E. DROM

21. The part of the CPU which directs the sequence of instructions and flow of data is the

21.____

    A. ALU   B. control unit   C. memory
    D. logic unit   E. arithmetic unit

22. _____ is the placement on disk or tape of two or more consecutive records in between interblock gaps.

22.____

    A. Gapping   B. Blocking   C. Staggering
    D. Sequencing   E. Sorting

23. When updating a sequential file,

23.____

    A. *only* the record being updated is changed
    B. *only* the record and those preceding it are changed
    C. the entire file must be read and rewritten
    D. *only* the record being updated and those following it are changed
    E. two new files are created

24. Sequential files are used PRIMARILY for

24.____

    A. backup data   B. on-line processing
    C. interactive processing   D. timesharing
    E. all of the above

25. In a hierarchial database, data is stored in a _____ relationship.

25.____

    A. father-son   B. member-owner   C. sequential
    D. direct   E. none of the above

KEY (CORRECT ANSWERS)

1.	B		11.	B
2.	C		12.	D
3.	D		13.	E
4.	C		14.	C
5.	E		15.	C
6.	C		16.	C
7.	D		17.	E
8.	B		18.	B
9.	A		19.	E
10.	D		20.	A

21.	B
22.	B
23.	C
24.	A
25.	B

———————

TEST 2

DIRECTIONS: Each question or incomplete statement is followed by several suggested answers or completions. Select the one that BEST answers the question or completes the statement. *PRINT THE LETTER OF THE CORRECT ANSWER IN THE SPACE AT THE RIGHT.*

1. The _____ communication line allows the short distance (50-75 miles) transmission of data through the airwaves.

    A. satellite   B. fiber-optics   C. laser
    D. microwave   E. coaxial

1.____

2. _____ data transmission permits *only* one character to be transmitted at a time.

    A. Full duplex   B. Half duplex   C. Asynchronous
    D. Parallel   E. Simplex

2.____

3. During _____, the computer *asks* a terminal if it has data to process.

    A. polling   B. surveying   C. inquiry
    D. dialing   E. calling

3.____

4. _____ is a centralized type of computer network used on larger computer systems.

    A. LAN   B. Star network
    C. Ring network   D. Distributed network
    E. All of the above

4.____

5. An advantage of low-level languages over high-level languages is that low-level languages

    A. are easier to write in
    B. are easier to find and correct errors
    C. can make optimum use of computer resources
    D. need very few instructions to write a complete program
    E. all of the above are advantages

5.____

6. The software to be loaded FIRST before any other software can be loaded into the computer is the

    A. applications program   B. utility programs
    C. operating system   D. compilers
    E. programming languages

6.____

7. Which of the following is NOT an operating system?

    A. OS/VS   B. MS-DOS   C. UNIX
    D. OS2   E. Cobol

7.____

8. A _____ graphically describes the flow of data through a system.

    A. data flow diagram   B. hierarchy chart
    C. pseudocode   D. HIPO chart
    E. Gantt chart

8.____

9. A list of the files, records, fields, etc. used in a system is maintained in a   9.____

    A. program maintenance notebook
    B. data dictionary
    C. system documentation manual
    D. operator's manual
    E. transaction log

10. A(n) _____ is generated by a computerized business system to track accounting trans- 10.____
actions back to their source.

    A. transaction log   B. data dictionary
    C. audit trail   D. system flowchart
    E. all of the above

11. A _____ is used to schedule the time it will take to complete computer tasks or program   11.____
development.

    A. system flowchart   B. data flow diagram
    C. Gantt chart   D. data dictionary
    E. transaction log

12. Which conversion method is used for converting a manual system to a computerized   12.____
system?

    A. Parallel   B. Direct
    C. Test-site   D. All of the above
    E. None of the above

13. The organization responsible for the standardization of programming languages and pro- 13.____
cedures is

    A. NCAA   B. ANSI   C. NCAP   D. CODASYL   E. DLL

14. The process whereby a program is reviewed step by step in an effort to uncover flaws in   14.____
the program is called

    A. flowcharting   B. pseudocode
    C. structured walkthrough   D. IPO
    E. data flow diagramming

15. Which of the following is an application for personal computers?   15.____

    A. Word processing
    B. Electronic spreadsheets
    C. Database management systems
    D. Computerized accounting systems
    E. All of the above

16. Which of the following is an entry-level position?   16.____

    A. Analyst   B. Applications programmer
    C. Systems programmer   D. Database administrator
    E. Lead programmer

17. *Computer security* refers to protection from

    A.   unauthorized users
    B.   abusive users
    C.   misuse of computer resources
    D.   disasters such as fire and flood
    E.   all of the above

17.____

18. The process of transforming a telephone (analog) to a computer (digital) signal so that it may be understood by the computer system is called

    A.   modulation   B.   demodulation   C.   analogation
    D.   digitalization   E.   multiplexing

18.____

19. The _____ computer numbering system uses both number and letter symbols to represent values.

    A.   binary   B.   digital   C.   decimal
    D.   octal   E.   hexadecimal

19.____

20. One type of computer file contains data that is relatively *static,* that is, data that does not change on a regular basis. This file is treated as an authority on records which are associated with it.
This paragraph BEST describes a(n) _____ file.

    A.   transaction   B.   index   C.   master
    D.   memory   E.   authority

20.____

21. A _____ is a set of rules which governs the transmission of data over a communications channel.

    A.   protocol   B.   handshake   C.   sequencer
    D.   modem   E.   algorithm

21.____

22. This technique is used to transmit large quantities of data from the CPU to tape or disk so that it can be output through a low-speed device such as a printer. The CPU is then free to process other data.
This paragraph BEST describes the process of

    A.   modulation   B.   demodulation
    C.   spooling   D.   updating
    E.   transaction processing

22.____

23. One type of computer memory uses disk or tape to store portions of software not in use. With this type of memory, the computer has almost unlimited main memory capacity.
This paragraph BEST describes

    A.   VLSI   B.   VSAM
    C.   virtual memory   D.   partioned memory
    E.   dynamic memory

23.____

24. *Throughput* measures computer

    A.   memory capacity
    B.   storage capacity

24.____

C. speed at which work can be processed
D. CPU speed
E. all of the above

25. EBCDIC, ASCII, and Hollerith code are all   25._____

A. hexadecimal codes
B. binary codes
C. zoned coding systems
D. used on magnetic storage devices (disk and tape)
E. used to represent numeric values only

KEY (CORRECT ANSWERS)

1.	D		11.	C
2.	C		12.	D
3.	A		13.	B
4.	B		14.	C
5.	C		15.	E
6.	C		16.	B
7.	E		17.	E
8.	A		18.	A
9.	B		19.	E
10.	C		20.	C

21. A
22. C
23. C
24. C
25. C

EXAMINATION SECTION
TEST 1

DIRECTIONS: Each question or incomplete statement is followed by several suggested
answers or completions. Select the one that BEST answers the question or
completes the statement. *PRINT THE LETTER OF THE CORRECT ANSWER
IN THE SPACE AT THE RIGHT.*

1. Which of the following ASCII codes corresponds to the character *1?*   1.____

    A. 061   B. 100   C. 101   D. 361

2. Generally, the FIRST step in designing a data processing system is to   2.____

    A. draft a HIPO diagram
    B. select input/output and file descriptors
    C. draft a flowchart
    D. select the processing method

3. A(n) _____ is the term for any signal or message that indicates the receipt of data or   3.____
    commands.

    A. indicator   B. concession
    C. address   D. acknowledgement

4. Which of the following aspects of data handling are MOST expensive?   4.____

    A. Validation and protection
    B. Storage and retrieval
    C. Collection and transcription
    D. Organization and aggregation

5. The flowchart drawing shown at the right represents a _____ symbol.   5.____

    A. display
    B. document
    C. off-line storage
    D. connector

6. What is the term for the reduction of a mass of data to a manageable form?   6.____

    A. Compression   B. File restructuring
    C. Summarizing   D. Aggregation

7. In _____ processing, data is handled as soon as it is available.   7.____

    A. simultaneous   B. batch
    C. distributed   D. transaction

8. Which of the following is a linear data list in which elements are added and removed only   8.____
    from one end of the list?

    A. Stack   B. String   C. Queue   D. B-tree

9. When four binary digits are read as a single number, the _____ numbering system is being used.   9.____

    A. shorthand   B. quaternary
    C. decimal   D. hexadecimal

10. A company uses its data processing system to prepare a reminder notice for a customer whose payment deadline has passed.   10.____
This is an example of

    A. summarization   B. control-break reporting
    C. issuance   D. selection

11. In an array with columns numbered from 4 through 13 and rows from 6 through 12, the MAXIMUM number of elements that can be stored is   11.____

    A. 56   B. 63   C. 70   D. 144

12. The symbol shown at the right represents a(n)   12.____

    A. *OR* gate
    B. inverter
    C. *NOR* gate
    D. *NAND* gate

13. When data is accessed from a database in response to an application program request, which of the following occurs FIRST?   13.____

    A. Data element is accessed and stored in a buffer of the database management system (DBMS).
    B. DBMS issues command to access data from secondary storage.
    C. Control unit transfers control to the DBMS.
    D. DBMS transfers data element to application program storage area.

14. An *interrupt* is   14.____

    A. a notation to the control unit that a condition has arisen that requires attention
    B. the arrest of data processing due to bit error
    C. the primary means by which a technician isolates computer failures
    D. an internal command which causes the computer to cease operation

15. In certain internal sort algorithms, the next logically sequential key in an unsorted list is chosen and placed in the next position in a growing sorted list.   15.____
What is the term for this type of sort?

    A. Stable   B. Selection
    C. Sequential   D. Partition-exchange sort

16. A(n) _____ is NOT classified as a *simple* logical data structure.   16.____

    A. array   B. record   C. graph   D. string

17. Each of the following is a component of a control unit EXCEPT a   17.____

    A. compiler   B. register
    C. decoder   D. program counter

18. A data report shows information on the sales of a single product, with three subtotals and a grand total.
This is an example of

    A. information retrieval   B. control-break reporting
    C. updating   D. summarizing

18.____

19. Which of the following rules applies to a computer's *AND* gate?
The output is

    A. inactive only if all inputs are active
    B. active if any one of the inputs is active
    C. active only if all inputs are active
    D. inactive if any one of the inputs is active

19.____

20. A _____ is a data collision resolution technique in which a search for an empty location proceeds serially from the record's home address.

    A. collating sequence   B. double hashing
    C. multigraphing   D. linear probing

20.____

21. When a unit needs further information to define the required operation, that information is typically held in the

    A. register   B. control word
    C. instructions   D. memory

21.____

22. Each of the following is a typical application of stacks EXCEPT

    A. identifying windows in a screen management system
    B. inventory lists
    C. selecting the next packet to be processed from a communications line
    D. menu picks in a hierarchical menu system

22.____

23. Which of the following is represented by the flowchart symbol shown at the right?

    A. Connector symbol
    B. Manual action symbol
    C. Flow lines
    D. Communications-link symbol

23.____

24. The MAIN advantage associated with having a head node on a data list is

    A. conservation of space
    B. help in finding the end of a circular list
    C. improved performance when finding a node prior to any node on the list
    D. improved performance when deleting nodes from the list

24.____

25. In octal code, the binary number 101 111 011 would appear as

    A. 243   B. 7F   C. 573   D. DR

25.____

KEY (CORRECT ANSWERS)

1.	A		11.	C
2.	B		12.	D
3.	D		13.	C
4.	C		14.	A
5.	A		15.	B
6.	C		16.	C
7.	D		17.	A
8.	A		18.	B
9.	D		19.	C
10.	C		20.	D

21.	B
22.	C
23.	D
24.	B
25.	C

———

TEST 2

DIRECTIONS: Each question or incomplete statement is followed by several suggested answers or completions. Select the one that BEST answers the question or completes the statement. *PRINT THE LETTER OF THE CORRECT ANSWER IN THE SPACE AT THE RIGHT.*

1. A customer withdraws $200 from her checking account at an automated teller machine, and that amount is immediately deducted from her account balance.
    This is an example of

    A. multi-key processing   B. control-break reporting
    C. real-time processing   D. data packing

    1.____

2. The quantity of characters in a data numbering system are denoted by the system's

    A. radix   B. code   C. array   D. digits

    2.____

3. Each of the following is an example of *linear* logical data structure EXCEPT

    A. linked list   B. queue
    C. general tree   D. stack

    3.____

4. Which basic computer element is represented by the symbol shown at the right?

    A. NOR gate
    B. Inverter
    C. Exclusive OR gate
    D. AND gate

    4.____

5. _____ is a technique for managing records on storage where a record's key value is mapped to an area of space that can hold multiple records.

    A. Cylinder addressing   B. Bucket addressing
    C. Multi-key processing   D. Sector addressing

    5.____

6. When a computer receives a halt instruction, each of the following is true EXCEPT the

    A. instruction-address counter holds the address of the next instruction to be executed
    B. results of the instruction executed prior to the halt instruction are left undisturbed by the halt instruction
    C. computer will not resume operation without manual intervention
    D. memory automatically stores the results of the instruction executed prior to the halt instruction

    6.____

7. When a binary operator appears between its operands, it is said to be using the _____ notation method of representing an arithmetic expression.

    A. prefix   B. postfix
    C. insertion sort   D. infix

    7.____

8. When data can be accessed without reference to previous data, the _____ access method is in effect.

    A. direct   B. sequential
    C. cross-keyed   D. indexed

    8.____

9. The purpose of a HIPO diagram is to

    A. organize the instructions within a routine or subroutine
    B. map out the physical components of a data processing system
    C. prioritize the instructions involved in storage and retrieval of data items
    D. list the steps involved in taking identified inputs and creating required files or out-puts

   9.__

10. A librarian keys in the title of a book on a display terminal to see whether it has been checked out.
This is an example of

    A. sorting
    C. issuance
    B. information retrieval
    D. distributed processing

   10.__

11. What is the term for unselective copying of memory contents to another storage medium?

    A. Dump   B. Rush   C. Scratch   D. Filigree

   11.__

12. What is the term for the data structure that is a finite sequence of symbols taken from a character set?

    A. List   B. Queue   C. String   D. Stack

   12.__

13. Which of the following types of numbering systems is a shorthand method for replacing a group of three binary digits with a single digit?

    A. Tertiary
    C. Hexadecimal
    B. Octal
    D. Triplex

   13.__

14. When two unequal key values map to the same data address, _____ occurs.

    A. bubble sorting
    C. a collision
    B. concatenation
    D. inversion

   14.__

15. A bank records all deposits made to customer accounts at the end of each work day.
This is an example of

    A. batch processing
    C. distributed processing
    B. hashing
    D. control-break reporting

   15.__

16. Each of the following is held in a computer's primary memory EXCEPT

    A. programs and data that have been passed to the computer for processing
    B. machine-language instructions
    C. output that is ready to be transmitted to an output device
    D. intermediate processing results

   16.__

17. *Pushing* and *popping* data are terms used in reference to which data structure?

    A. Strings   B. Queues   C. B-trees   D. Stacks

   17.__

18. Which of the following methods for file access makes use of fields which are used to identify each record in the file?

    A. Keyed
    C. Sequential
    B. Distributed
    D. Direct

   18.__

19. Each of the following is an example of a *primitive* logical data structure EXCEPT   19.____

    A. character   B. list   C. boolean   D. integer

20. In hexadecimal code, the number 1110 1111 would appear as   20.____

    A. 6A   B. 116   C. EF   D. 192

21. Which of the following is a data collision resolution stragegy in which synonyms for a   21.____
record are all stored in the file's primary address space?

    A. Separate-overflow addressing
    B. Linear probing
    C. Open addressing
    D. Double hashing

22. Typically, the jobs to be performed by a system, as well as the programs that will perform   22.____
them, are controlled and selected by the

    A. subroutine   B. executive program
    C. compiler   D. directory

23. In a computer's *NOR* gate, the output is inactive   23.____

    A. *only* if all inputs are inactive
    B. if any one input is inactive
    C. *only* if all inputs are active
    D. if any one input is active

24. A company uses its data processing system to compose an employee phone book with   24.____
names in alphabetical order.
This is an example of

    A. sorting   B. b-tree hierarchy
    C. selection   D. issuance

25. Which of the following components of the arithmetic unit is capable of performing logical   25.____
operations?

    A. Compiler   B. Carry-in   C. Counter   D. Adder

KEY (CORRECT ANSWERS)

1.	C		11.	A
2.	A		12.	C
3.	C		13.	B
4.	C		14.	C
5.	B		15.	A
6.	D		16.	B
7.	D		17.	D
8.	A		18.	A
9.	D		19.	B
10.	B		20.	C

21. C
22. B
23. D
24. A
25. D

———

EXAMINATION SECTION
TEST 1

DIRECTIONS: Each question or incomplete statement is followed by several suggested answers or completions. Select the one that BEST answers the question or completes the statement. *PRINT THE LETTER OF THE CORRECT ANSWER IN THE SPACE AT THE RIGHT.*

1. Files are used to store   1.____

    A. data   B. programs
    C. operating systems   D. source programs
    E. all of the above

2. MOST hard disks hold _____ bytes.   2.____

    A. 1-100 trillion   B. 1-100 billion   C. 1-100 million
    D. 1-1000   E. less than 1000

3. MOST floppy disks can store _____ bytes.   3.____

    A. 1-100 trillion   B. 1-100 billion   C. 1-100 million
    D. 1-1 million   E. less than 1000

4. A master file stores   4.____

    A. data about particular events
    B. relatively permanent data
    C. source copies of programs
    D. copies of other files
    E. data extracted from another file and held for a short term

5. A transaction file stores   5.____

    A. data about particular events
    B. relatively permanent data
    C. source copies of programs
    D. copies of other files
    E. data extracted from another file and held for a short term

6. A program file stores   6.____

    A. data about particular events
    B. relatively permanent data
    C. source copies of programs
    D. copies of other files
    E. data extracted from another file and held for a short term

7. A backup file stores   7.____

    A. data about particular events
    B. relatively permanent data
    C. source copies of programs
    D. copies of other files
    E. data extracted from another file and held for a short term

8. Which of the following is NOT a type of storage method? 8.__

   A. EBCDIC   B. Packed hexadecimal
   C. Packed decimal D. True binary
   E. ASCII

9. Which of the following is the storage method commonly used by IBM? 9.__

   A. EBCDIC   B. Packed hexadecimal
   C. Packed decimal D. True binary
   E. ASCII

10. Which of the following is a very efficient numerical storage method? 10.__

   A. EBCDIC   B. Packed hexadecimal
   C. Packed decimal D. True binary
   E. ASCII

11. Which of the following is the type of storage method commonly found on home or personal computers, as well as many mini-computers? 11.__

   A. EBCDIC   B. Packed hexadecimal
   C. Packed decimal D. True binary
   E. ASCII

12. In the EBCDIC storage method, 12.__

   A. numbers follow letters
   B. letters follow numbers
   C. numbers are intermixed with letters
   D. numbers cannot be stored
   E. letters cannot be stored

13. In the ASCII storage method, 13.__

   A. numbers follow letters
   B. letters follow numbers
   C. numbers are intermixed with letters
   D. numbers cannot be stored
   E. letters cannot be stored

14. The collating sequence refers to 14.__

   A. the order of the letters in the alphabet
   B. the order of the digits 0 through 9
   C. the order of manufacturers of computers
   D. the order of numbers and letters relative to each other
   E. none of the above

15. A two-letter state abbreviation takes how many bytes of computer memory when stored in ASCII? 15.__

   A. 0   B. 1   C. 2
   D. 5   E. None of the above

16. A two-letter state abbreviation takes how many bytes of computer memory when stored in EBCDIC?   16.____

    A. 0   B. 1   C. 2
    D. 5   E. None of the above

17. An alternative to storing numeric data in EBCDIC is to store it in   17.____

    A. ZIP format   B. true trinary   C. true hexabinary
    D. true binary   E. all of the above

18. Packed decimal means each decimal digit is stored in   18.____

    A. one nibble   B. one byte   C. ASCII format
    D. EBCDIC format   E. all of the above

19. Generally speaking, alphanumeric data should be stored in   19.____

    A. nibbles   B. straight binary   C. EBCDIC
    D. packed decimal   E. all of the above

20. Which statement below BEST describes a capability associated with virtual storage?   20.____

    A. It is possible to program as if more core is available than exists in the system
    B. All computers are now automatically compatible
    C. Only tapes and disks can be used for storage
    D. The programmer can write efficient programs while completely ignoring the nature of the computer system being used
    E. None of the above

KEY (CORRECT ANSWERS)

1.	A	11.	E
2.	C	12.	A
3.	D	13.	B
4.	B	14.	D
5.	A	15.	C
6.	C	16.	C
7.	D	17.	D
8.	B	18.	A
9.	A	19.	C
10.	D	20.	A

TEST 2

DIRECTIONS: Each question or incomplete statement is followed by several suggested answers or completions. Select the one that BEST answers the question or completes the statement. *PRINT THE LETTER OF THE CORRECT ANSWER IN THE SPACE AT THE RIGHT.*

1. Which of the following is NOT a common tape density?   1.___

     A.   800   B.   1600   C.   2400   D.   6250
     E.   All are common densities

2. Which of the following is a common tape length?   2.___

     A.   800   B.   1600   C.   2400   D.   6250
     E.   All are common densities

3. Blocking refers to the   3.___

     A.   number of physical records in a logical record
     B.   number of bytes in a record
     C.   number of bytes per inch of tape
     D.   number of logical records in a physical record
     E.   the space between physical records

4. The inter block gap refers to the   4.___

     A.   number of physical records in a logical record
     B.   number of bytes in a record
     C.   number of bytes per inch of tape
     D.   number of logical records in a physical record
     E.   the space between physical records

5. Density refers to the   5.___

     A.   number of physical records in a logical record
     B.   number of bytes in a record
     C.   number of bytes per inch of tape
     D.   number of logical records in a physical record
     E.   the space between physical records

6. The record length refers to the   6.___

     A.   number of physical records in a logical record
     B.   number of bytes in a record
     C.   number of bytes per inch of tape
     D.   number of logical records in a physical record
     E.   the space between physical records

7. Disks are BEST used in situations where   7.___

     A.   we need to store ineexpensively
     B.   we need to store historical data
     C.   we want to process data sequentially
     D.   we need to store data for on-line applications
     E.   All of the above

8. Tape is BEST used in situations where   8.____

    A. we need to store data inexpensively
    B. we need to store historical data
    C. we want to process data sequentially
    D. we do not need to store data for on-line applications
    E. All of the above

9. Which of the following is NOT a direct access method?   9.____

    A. VSAM
    B. Sequential
    C. KSAM
    D. ISAM
    E. All of the above are direct access methods

10. A basing algorithm calculates a records location in a file using a(n)   10.____

    A. record address
    B. social security number
    C. key field like a social security number
    D. using the binary search strategy
    E. all of the above

11. The soundex algorithm converts   11.____

    A. numeric keys to disk addresses
    B. disk addresses to numeric keys
    C. disk addresses to alphanumeric keys
    D. alphanumeric keys to disk addresses
    E. disk addresses to collisions

12. A collision occurs if two records have the   12.____

    A. same record key
    B. hash to the same disk address
    C. same length
    D. same blocking factor
    E. same density

13. In designing a tape file, an analyst should consider which of the following factors?   13.____

    A. Record fields
    B. Sequential order of records
    C. Estimate the number of records in the file
    D. Calculate the record length
    E. All of the above

14. In designing a tape file, an analyst should consider which of the following factors?   14.____

    A. Order of fields in a record
    B. Placement of fields in a record
    C. An expansion area for future use
    D. Data storage method, EBCDIC or packed decimal
    E. All of the above

15. A record count tallies the number of   15.____

    A. records in the file
    B. number of fields in each record
    C. number of bytes in a record
    D. files in the database
    E. All of the above

16. The term backup means   16.____

    A. copying each record to a new record
    B. copying a file to tape
    C. copying a disk to memory
    D. deleting a file from disk
    E. deleting a file from a tape

17. The interblock gap is typically _____ inch(es).   17.____

    A. .05   B. .005   C. .5   D. 5   E. 50

18. In writing the schema, the analyst defines   18.____

    A. data sets
    B. data elements
    C. data type, numeric or alphanumeric
    D. slave data sets
    E. All of the above

19. Which of the following is a typical data manipulation language command?   19.____

    A. QUERY   B. LOCK   C. DML
    D. DDL   E. None of the above

20. Which of the following statements concerning index files and backup programs is TRUE?   20.____

    A. Index files may not be backed up.
    B. All appropriate index files are automatically backed up whenever a database file backup is created.
    C. Index files are often not backed up because they are so easily rebuilt.
    D. Index files must be backed up whenever their database files are backed up.
    E. None of the above

KEY (CORRECT ANSWERS)

1.	B	11.	D
2.	C	12.	B
3.	D	13.	E
4.	E	14.	E
5.	C	15.	A
6.	B	16.	B
7.	D	17.	C
8.	E	18.	E
9.	B	19.	B
10.	C	20.	C

EXAMINATION SECTION
TEST 1

DIRECTIONS: Each question or incomplete statement is followed by several suggested answers or completions. Select the one that *BEST* answers the question or completes the statement. *PRINT THE LETTER OF THE CORRECT ANSWER IN THE SPACE AT THE RIGHT.*

1. A word processor   1._____

    A.   requires that typing and printing take place at the same time
    B.   can be programmed to automatically check for spelling errors
    C.   uses more carbon paper and ink than a typewriter
    D.   prints more slowly than a good typist but produces clearer copies

2. On a word processor, a *cursor*   2._____

    A.   types the text as you go along
    B.   indicates where you are on the screen
    C.   scans the keyboard
    D.   clears the screen

3. Flow charts   3._____

    A.   monitor the hydraulic pressure in the computer
    B.   indicate the location of computers in an organizational structure
    C.   outline the structure of a program
    D.   portray statistical data graphically

4. Floppy disks   4._____

    A.   can be single sided or double sided
    B.   can be 5 1/4" wide or 8" wide
    C.   can be single density or double density
    D.   all of the above

5. Which of the following is a random-access storage device?   5._____

    A.   Magnetic tape   B.   Modem
    C.   RAM   D.   Public library

6. Integrated circuits have replaced transistors which replaced   6._____

    A.   wires   B.   vacuum tubes
    C.   crystals   D.   magnets

7. Microcomputer memory is usually expressed in thousands (for example, *64K*) of   7._____

    A.   bits   B.   bytes
    C.   words   D.   instructions

8. A computer program is originally stored   8._____

    A.   *internally* during execution
    B.   *externally* during execution
    C.   *internally* after execution
    D.   *inside* the algorithm

9. The NOR gate is an inverted _____ gate.   9.____

   A. OR   B. AND   C. XOR   D. NAND

10. When soldering FET devices, the soldering iron should have the tip grounded to prevent   10.____

   A. static charge   B. heat buildup
   C. solder set   D. fusing

11. Which is *smallest?*   11.____

   A. Microsecond   B. Millisecond
   C. Second   D. Nanosecond

12. Machine language programs   12.____

   A. consist of binary digits
   B. can be moved from one kind of computer to another
   C. are translated by compilers
   D. look like English

13. DC voltage has a _____ polarity.   13.____

   A. reversed   B. varied   C. signal   D. fixed

14. *Embedded commands* refer to   14.____

   A. punctuation marks in text you are typing
   B. subliminal messages which flash on the screen
   C. date, title, and other information related to identifying various files on a disk
   D. instructions for printing and formating test

15. In many disk drives, a 50 ms delay occurs when turning the power on so that   15.____

   A. there is time enough to turn on the LED
   B. the DC drive motor can come up to speed
   C. all the ICs (integrated circuits) receive line voltage
   D. the diskette will not jam in the machine and lose data

16. Electron flow through a diode is from   16.____

   A. anode to cathode
   B. anode 1 to anode 2
   C. cathode 1 to cathode 2
   D. cathode to anode

17. Bit is   17.____

   A. the colloquial term for byte
   B. a contraction of binary digit
   C. a contraction of basic iteration
   D. an abbreviation for *basic interaction terminal*

18. The abbreviation *DOS* refers to   18.____

   A. a program in computer memory which controls disk functions
   B. a special type of hard-disk drive

    C.   a popular commercial program for word processing

    D.   *Drive-oriented Software* that reduces the amount of required memory

19.   Which is not a binary number?   19._____

    A. 0   B. 1   C. 2   D. 10

20.   Which is not an octal number?   20._____

    A. 777   B. 010   C. 234   D. 999

DIRECTIONS: In questions 21-30 choose the *two* answers that are associated with the terms in the question.

21.   dot matrix, letter quality   21._____

    A.   Output devices   B.   Flow charts   C.   Memory devices

    D.   Printers   E.   Computer file commands

22.   Which of the following abbreviations are commonly used in computer technology?   22._____

    A.   CPU   B.   QID   C.   ETC

    D.   CRT   E.   AMA

23.   RAM, ROM   23._____

    A.   Input devices   B.   Memory devices

    C.   Main-frame computers   D.   Microcomputers

    E.   Computer languages

24.   Data transmission, teleprocessing   24._____

    A.   modem   B.   baud rate   C.   BPI

    D.   CAT scanner   E.   teletransportation

25.   interactive, time-sharing   25._____

    A.   remote terminals   B.   batch processing

    C.   more than one user   D.   analog computers

    E.   binary service

26.   floating point, integer   26._____

    A.   control statements   B.   numbers   C.   loops

    D.   exponentials   E.   integrated circuits

27.   FORTRAN, PASCAL   27._____

    A.   languages   B.   peripherals   C.   compilers

    D.   assemblers   E.   flow charts

28.   A computer programmer may use which of the following: 28._____

    A.   typewriter keyboard   B.   laser

    C.   cathode ray tube   D.   x-ray tube

    E.   soldering iron

29. The POKE function   29.____

    A. assigns a value or a variable to a memory location
    B. can be put into RAM only
    C. can be put into RAM or ROM
    D. lets you *peek* at any memory location
    E. lets you assign subroutines to specific memory locations

30. assembler, compiler   30.____

    A. software   B. CPU
    C. peripherals   D. produce machine language
    E. line printer

KEY (CORRECT ANSWERS)

1.	B	11.	D	21.	A-D
2.	B	12.	A	22.	A-D
3.	C	13.	D	23.	B-D
4.	D	14.	D	24.	A-B
5.	C	15.	B	25.	A-C
6.	B	16.	A	26.	B-D
7.	B	17.	B	27.	A-C
8.	A	18.	A	28.	A-C
9.	A	19.	C	29.	A-B
10.	A	20.	D	30.	A-D

EXAMINATION SECTION

TEST 1

DIRECTIONS: Each question or incomplete statement is followed by several suggested answers or completions. Select the one that BEST answers the question or completes the statement. *PRINT THE LETTER OF THE CORRECT ANSWER IN THE SPACE AT THE RIGHT.*

1. Shortcut keys can be used for
   A. navigation
   B. software
   C. formatting text
   D. all of the above

   1._____

2. A basic keyboard has _____ types of keys.
   A. 4
   B. 6
   C. 3
   D. none of the above

   2._____

3. Which combination of keys is used to switch among opened programs?
   A. Ctrl+Tab
   B. Alt+Tab+Del
   C. Shift+Alt
   D. Both A and B

   3._____

4. To insert hyperlink for selected text, which shortcut key is used?
   A. Ctrl+P
   B. Ctrl+O
   C. Ctrl+K
   D. All of the above

   4._____

5. Pressing the Ctrl and Home keys together clears the screen and sends the cursor to the
   A. top of the document or page
   B. previous page
   C. next page
   D. header of the document

   5._____

6. Which keys are used to open the Start menu in Microsoft Windows?
   A. Windows
   B. Ctrl+Esc
   C. Ctrl+Tab
   D. Both A and B

   6._____

7. The separate keys for letters, numbers and special characters are known as
   A. character keys
   B. special
   C. functional
   D. hot keys

   7._____

8. Which of the following keys perform customized functions for different software?
   A. Special
   B. Functional
   C. Character
   D. None of the above

   8._____

9. To lock or log off Windows, which combination of keys is used?
   A. Windows + L
   B. Windows + M
   C. Windows + S
   D. All of the above

   9._____

10. A dialogue box is opened when _____ is pressed together.   10.____
     A. Windows + R   B. Windows + O
     C. Ctrl + O   D. Ctrl + P

11. This symbol (-) on a keyboard is known as a   11.____
     A. dash   B. hyphen
     C. minus   D. slash

12. This symbol (') on a keyboard is known as a(n)   12.____
     A. apostrophe   B. semicolon
     C. comma   D. ampersand

13. Three periods (...) written in a sentence are called a(n)   13.____
     A. full stop   B. dash
     C. ellipsis   D. em dash

14. Which of the following are known as angle brackets?   14.____
     A. ()   B. {}
     C. <>   D. all of the above

15. The forward slash (/) is commonly found on the same key as the   15.____
     A. exclamation point   B. period
     C. comma   D. question mark

16. Special characters are typed by pressing numeric keys along with the   16.____
_____ key.
     A. Alt   B. Ctrl
     C. Shift   D. all of the above

17. To type an open and closed parentheses, you would press 9 and 0 while holding   17.____
the _____ key.
     A. Shift   B. Ctrl
     C. Tab   D. command

18. Which combination of keys is required to display the dollar sign ($)?   18.____
     A. Shift + 4   B. Ctrl + 4
     C. Alt + 4   D. Both A and B

19. In standard keyboarding, the pointer fingers are positioned on the __ and __ keys.   19.____
     A. F, J   B. G, J
     C. D, K   D. S, L

20. Which of the following words will usually be typed with the left hand only?   20.____
     A. Fire   B. Free
     C. True   D. Tired

21. Which of the following symbols can be typed without the use of the Shift key?   21.____
     A. Pound sign   B. Percent sign
     C. Semicolon   D. Colon

22. The _____ currency symbol is displayed when Alt+0128 is pressed.   22.____
    A. dollar   B. pound
    C. Euro   D. none of the above

23. Alt+0149 is pressed to display a _____ symbol.   23.____
    A. •   B. -
    C. ;   D. $

24. The special character for copyright is denoted by   24.____
    A. ©   B. @
    C. ¥   D. both A and B

25. Alt+0174 is a key combination to display the special character for   25.____
    A. registered trademark   B. copyright
    C. both A and B   D. none of the above

KEY (CORRECT ANSWERS)

1.	D		11.	B
2.	A		12.	A
3.	A		13.	C
4.	C		14.	C
5.	A		15.	D
6.	D		16.	A
7.	A		17.	A
8.	B		18.	D
9.	A		19.	A
10.	A		20.	B

21.	C
22.	C
23.	A
24.	A
25.	A

TEST 2

DIRECTIONS: Each question or incomplete statement is followed by several suggested answers or completions. Select the one that BEST answers the question or completes the statement. *PRINT THE LETTER OF THE CORRECT ANSWER IN THE SPACE AT THE RIGHT.*

1. Common control keys are
   A. Home
   B. Escape
   C. Delete
   D. all of the above

   1.____

2. The numeric keypad is useful for
   A. business environment
   B. data entry
   C. accounts
   D. all of the above

   2.____

3. In the keyboard, mechanical key switches include the
   A. rubber dome
   B. metal contact
   C. foam element
   D. all of the above

   3.____

4. To create a shortcut of the selected item, which key combination is required?
   A. Ctrl+Shift
   B. Ctrl+Alt
   C. Alt+Shift
   D. All of the above

   4.____

5. If a file or folder is needed to search, the _____ key works well.
   A. F4
   B. F11
   C. F3
   D. none of the above

   5.____

6. Properties for the selected item can be seen while pressing
   A. Alt+Enter
   B. Alt+F4
   C. Alt+O
   D. all of the above

   6.____

7. The shortcut menu for the selected item is displayed when _____ are pressed together.
   A. Shift+Alt
   B. Shift+F10
   C. both A and B
   D. none of the above

   7.____

8. The Ctrl+Shift+Tab combination is used to switch between opened programs in _____ direction.
   A. left
   B. right
   C. both A and B
   D. none of the above

   8.____

9. Alt+F4 closes all opened windows to show the desktop, whereas _____ shows the desktop without closing any window.
   A. Alt+O
   B. Windows+D
   C. Alt+Shift
   D. none of the above

   9.____

10. If the Shift key is pressed five times, it will switch on or off the   10.____
   A. filter keys   B. toggle keys
   C. sticky keys   D. all of the above

11. The Ctrl+Windows+F key combination works for searching   11.____
   A. files   B. folders
   C. computers   D. all of the above

12. _____ is an easy way to open *My Computer*.   12.____
   A. Windows + E   B. Windows + O
   C. Both A and B   D. All of the above

13. (™) is a special character which is displayed as a result of pressing   13.____
   A. Alt+0153   B. Alt+018
   C. Alt+010   D. none of the above

14. Alt+0163 is used to show _____ currency.   14.____
   A. $ B. £
   C. £   D. none of the above

15. The ~ symbol is known as a   15.____
   A. tilde   B. hyphen
   C. both A and B   D. none of the above

16. Isolated sentences that are grammatically independent but have closely   16.____
   connected meanings are joined by using a
   A. colon   B. comma
   C. semicolon   D. all of the above

17. The inverted exclamation is shown by typing   17.____
   A. Alt+0161   B. Alt+173
   C. none of the above   D. both A and B

18. Which one of the following is a currency symbol?   18.____
   A. ¤   B. ¡
   C. ~   D. none of the above

19. Alt+58 displays the character   19.____
   A. "   B. :
   C. ,   D. none of the above

20. The logical not sign is denoted by   20.____
   A. ¬   B. ⎺
   C. both A and B   D. none of the above

21. The ¼ (one quarter) special character is displayed when _____ are pressed.   21._____
    A. Alt+172   B. Alt+0188
    C. both A and B   D. none of the above

22. The ⁻ symbol is known as a   22._____
    A. macron   B. hyphen
    C. dash   D. all of the above

23. Alt+19 is used to display   23._____
    A. !   B. ‼
    C. &   D. all of the above

24. For capital letters, which one of the following works well?   24._____
    A. Alt+65 to Alt+90   B. Shift + alphabets
    C. None of the above   D. Both A and B

25. The special character ¶ is shown when _____ is pressed.   25._____
    A. Alt+Tab   B. Alt+20
    C. Alt+0120   D. all of the above

KEY (CORRECT ANSWERS)

1.	D		11.	C
2.	D		12.	A
3.	D		13.	A
4.	A		14.	B
5.	C		15.	A
6.	A		16.	C
7.	B		17.	D
8.	A		18.	A
9.	B		19.	B
10.	C		20.	D

21.	C
22.	A
23.	B
24.	D
25.	B

TEST 3

DIRECTIONS: Each question or incomplete statement is followed by several suggested answers or completions. Select the one that BEST answers the question or completes the statement. *PRINT THE LETTER OF THE CORRECT ANSWER IN THE SPACE AT THE RIGHT.*

1. Which one of the following key combinations is used to open a new tab in the browser?   1._____
   A. Ctrl+Tab
   B. Ctrl+O
   C. Ctrl+T
   D. All of the above

2. Snapshot is taken when _____ is pressed together.   2._____
   A. Ctrl+Alt+S
   B. Ctrl+Shift+S
   C. Ctrl+Shift+C
   D. none of the above

3. Ctrl+Shift+Esc opens the   3._____
   A. task manager
   B. control panel
   C. menu
   D. none of the above

4. Which command is useful when a magnifier is required for zoom out?   4._____
   A. Windows+-
   B. Windows-+
   C. Both A and B
   D. None of the above

5. _____ makes all Windows transparent so the desktop could be seen.   5._____
   A. Windows+Alt
   B. Windows+Shift
   C. Windows+Space
   D. All of the above

6. Which key combination brings all gadgets on top and the forefront?   6._____
   A. Windows+G
   B. Windows+O
   C. Windows+P
   D. All of the above

7. _____ displays a preview thumbnail of running applications in the Windows taskbar one by one without mouse over.   7._____
   A. Shift+T
   B. Windows+T
   C. Windows+P
   D. All of the above

8. Windows+X opens windows   8._____
   A. mobility center
   B. help center
   C. both A and B
   D. all of the above

9. Windows+Shift+T cycles _____ in the taskbar.   9._____
   A. backward
   B. forward
   C. both A and B
   D. all of the above

10. The Windows+U key combination opens   10._____
    A. the control panel
    B. ease of access
    C. ease of access center
    D. all of the above

11. Which type of keys are included in the basic keyboard?
    A. Control keys   B. Function keys
    C. Navigation keys   D. All of the above

11.____

12. Rarely used keys on the keyboard are
    A. PrtScn   B. Scroll
    C. Pause   D. all of the above

12.____

13. _____ displays Windows help and support center.
    A. Shift+F1   B. Windows+F1
    C. Alt+F1   D. All of the above

13.____

14. When working with the help viewer, which key combination opens the table of contents?
    A. Alt+T   B. Alt+C
    C. Alt+O   D. All of the above

14.____

15. _____ displays the Option menu.
    A. F10   B. F2
    C. F11   D. None of the above

15.____

16. Alt+Home, when pressed together in the browser, opens up
    A. Menu   B. Start page
    C. none of the above   D. all of the above

16.____

17. Alt+A opens the _____ support page in the Help viewer.
    A. technical   B. customer
    C. help   D. all of the above

17.____

18. Fn+key is a combination for some symbols recognized by
    A. Windows   B. kernel
    C. operating system   D. both A and B

18.____

19. The Shift+Tab combination mostly helps out the _____ specialist.
    A. computer   B. data entry
    C. graphic   D. none of the above

19.____

20. Fn+F5 pressed together results in
    A. brightness down   B. brightness up
    C. close programs   D. none of the above

20.____

21. Which of the following keys are concerned with volume?
    A. Fn+F11   B. Fn+F12
    C. Fn+F10   D. All of the above

21.____

22. Which key combination closes the open window within the existing active window in Microsoft Windows?
    A. Shift+F4
    B. Alt+F4
    C. Ctrl+F4
    D. All of the above

22.____

23. _____ in Windows renames a highlighted icon, file, or folder in all types of Windows.
    A. F2
    B. F5
    C. F4
    D. None of the above

23.____

24. _____ will transform letters from upper to lower case or capitalize each word in Microsoft Word.
    A. Shift+F5
    B. Shift+F3
    C. None of the above
    D. Both A and B

24.____

25. In Microsoft Windows, F5 performs which of the following functions?
    A. Refresh pages in browser
    B. Show slideshow in Power Point
    C. Find and replace
    D. All of the above

25.____

KEY (CORRECT ANSWERS)

1.	C		11.	D
2.	B		12.	D
3.	A		13.	B
4.	A		14.	B
5.	C		15.	A
6.	A		16.	B
7.	B		17.	B
8.	A		18.	B
9.	A		19.	B
10.	C		20.	A

21. D
22. C
23. A
24. B
25. D

TEST 4

DIRECTIONS: Each question or incomplete statement is followed by several suggested answers or completions. Select the one that BEST answers the question or completes the statement. *PRINT THE LETTER OF THE CORRECT ANSWER IN THE SPACE AT THE RIGHT.*

1. Alt+double click displays the properties of the
   A. program   B. selected item
   C. none of the above   D. both A and B

   1.____

2. F1 frequently displays
   A. Windows help   B. Menu
   C. tool bar   D. all of the above

   2.____

3. _____ opens a shortcut menu for the selected item.
   A. Alt+F10   B. Shift+F10
   C. Both A and B   D. None of the above

   3.____

4. Ctrl+Esc and _____ do the same thing.
   A. Alt key   B. Windows key
   C. Fn key   D. Shift+Esc

   4.____

5. Press and hold down the _____ key while inserting a CD to avoid the automatic run function.
   A. Windows   B. Alt
   C. Shift   D. all of the above

   5.____

6. _____ closes the current multiple document interface (MDI) window.
   A. Alt+F4   B. Ctrl+F4
   C. Shift+F4   D. All of the above

   6.____

7. _____ switches between multiple windows in the same program.
   A. Alt+F6   B. Alt+F8
   C. Alt+Shift   D. None of the above

   7.____

8. Left Alt+left Shift + Num Lock will turn on and off
   A. filter keys   B. mouse keys
   C. both A and B   D. none of the above

   8.____

9. Windows+M and Windows+D _____ all opened programs.
   A. maximize   B. minimize
   C. close   D. none of the above

   9.____

10. _____ moves focus from start to the quick launch toolbar to the system tray.
    A. Ctrl+Tab+Windows   B. Ctrl+Windows+Tab
    C. Windows+Tab+Alt   D. All of the above

    10.____

11. _____ is equivalent to the Cancel command.
    A. Esc   B. Alt+F4
    C. Alt+Space   D. All of the above
11.____

12. _____ opens firebug or brower debug tool.
    A. Alt+F12   B. F12
    C. Shift+F12   D. All of the above
12.____

13. _____ access hidden recovery partitions in Dell and Lenovo computers.
    A. Shift+Alt   B. F11
    C. Alt   D. None of the above
13.____

14. Which functional key is accessed to go in hidden recovery partition in HP and Sony computers?
    A. Fn+F10   B. F10
    C. Shift+F10   D. All of the above
14.____

15. Which one of the following is used to enter in CMOS setup?
    A. F10   B. Fn+F10
    C. None of the above   D. Both A and B
15.____

16. In Microsoft Outlook, which key is used to send and receive email?
    A. Ctrl+S   B. Fn+F9
    C. F9   D. All of the above
16.____

17. Windows safe mode is accessed through
    A. F10   B. F8
    C. Fn+F10   D. none of the above
17.____

18. _____ shows a thumbnail image for all workspaces in Mac OS.
    A. F5   B. F9
    C. F8   D. None of the above
18.____

19. F8 is used to access Windows recovery system in _____ computers.
    A. Dell   B. some
    C. Sony   D. none of the above
19.____

20. In Microsoft programs, spell check and grammar check is performed by
    A. F7   B. Fn+F7
    C. both A and B   D. none of the above
20.____

21. _____ opens to another open Microsoft Word document.
    A. Shift+F6   B. Ctrl+Shift+F6
    C. Ctrl+Shift+F4   D. Ctrl+Shift+F5
21.____

22. In Firefox browser, _____ open clear data windows to quickly clear private data.

    A. Ctrl+Shift+Delete   B. Shift+Delete

    C. Ctrl+Delete   D. all of the above

22.____

23. Ctrl+J open up download windows in

    A. Firefox   B. Chrome

    C. both A and B   D. none of the above

23.____

24. _____ in Windows 8 opens the Start screen.

    A. Alt+S   B. Ctrl+Esc

    C. Ctrl+S   D. Both A and B

24.____

25. In all versions of Windows, _____ starts find or search at the Windows desktop.

    A. Ctrl+F3   B. F3

    C. Alt+F3   D. all of the above

25.____

KEY (CORRECT ANSWERS)

1.	B		11.	A
2.	A		12.	B
3.	B		13.	B
4.	B		14.	B
5.	C		15.	A
6.	A		16.	C
7.	A		17.	B
8.	B		18.	C
9.	B		19.	B
10.	B		20.	A

21.	B
22.	A
23.	C
24.	B
25.	B

EXAMINATION SECTION
TEST 1

DIRECTIONS: Each question or incomplete statement is followed by several suggested answers or completions. Select the one that BEST answers the question or completes the statement. *PRINT THE LETTER OF THE CORRECT ANSWER IN THE SPACE AT THE RIGHT.*

1. Suppose that an operator, assigned to you for supervision, refuses to accept an assignment which you give him.
   Of the following approaches, the one which you should usually try FIRST is to

   A. ask for an explanation for the refusal
   B. report the operator to your immediate supervisor
   C. find a co-worker to assist the operator with the work
   D. advise him that your position as supervisor allows you to enforce your requests

   1.____

2. Suppose that two of the operators whom you supervise have been bickering so consistently that it is disturbing other staff members.
   Of the following, the BEST action for you to take FIRST is to

   A. have one of them transferred to another office immediately
   B. have a meeting of the staff to discuss what action should be taken
   C. call each of the two operators into your office individually to discuss the problem
   D. call them to your office and tell them they will be transferred if their behavior does not improve

   2.____

3. A senior operator may often have to give instructions to a group of operators. When doing so, it is important that the instructions be correctly interpreted by all the operators.
   To insure this, it would be BEST for the senior operator to use words which are

   A. personal and emotionally directed
   B. slangy but diplomatic
   C. simple and easily understandable
   D. strong and authoritative

   3.____

4. Suppose that you, a supervisor in a unit, are told by management that certain major changes in the department may result in a big reshuffling of personnel in your unit, possibly even a reduction, but that you are to say nothing of this to anyone yet. The departmental grapevine is, however, spreading rumors of pending changes. One of the operators asks you directly what the plans are.
   Which of the following actions is BEST to take?

   A. Deny knowing anything and assure the operator that there is nothing to worry about.
   B. Tell this operator the truth, but swear her to strict secrecy.
   C. Inform this operator that the entire unit will be told the facts as soon as they are official.
   D. Advise the operator to resume her work and stop spreading rumors.

   4.____

5. Assume that you are the supervisor of a clerical unit which has a workload that fluctuates from day to day. You notice, while the rest of your staff is working, one of your workers has completed all the work you had assigned to her and is reading a magazine while her machine is idle. Generally, the BEST course of action for you to take is to   5.____

   A. ask her to read the magazine in a corner of the office where she is less noticeable to the other workers
   B. say nothing now, but make note of the incident for discussing it along with related matters at a later date
   C. overlook the situation since she is obviously a fast worker and deserves the rest
   D. give her more work to do, work which you had not originally included on her schedule

6. In supervising a unit, you may find it necessary to criticize the occasionally poor work of one of the operators.
   While criticizing the operator's work, it would usually be DESIRABLE for you to   6.____

   A. point out to her the good work she does, or has done, as well as her faults
   B. point out as many previous errors in her work as you can remember, to emphasize the need for this criticism
   C. end your criticism with a threat of more severe disciplinary action if her work does not improve
   D. end the criticism with friendliness by assuring the worker that you only brought the matter up because your supervisor told you to

7. Suppose that Sue Smith, an operator, who has always been a quiet and efficient worker, begins to talk back to Mary Jones, the senior operator, in a way that borders on insubordination. The quality of Sue Smith's work has begun to decline a little, but it is still good. What is the BEST thing that Mary Jones should do in these circumstances?   7.____

   A. Nothing, until the quality of Sue Smith's work shows a serious decline
   B. Keep reprimanding Sue Smith until she stops her back-talk
   C. Wait until Sue Smith is actually insubordinate and then recommend disciplinary action
   D. Talk to Sue Smith to find out why she has begun to act the way she has been

8. Suppose that you have found it necessary, for valid reasons, to criticize the work of one of the operators you supervise. She later comes to your desk and accuses you of picking on her work because you have resented her from the moment she was assigned to your unit.
   The BEST way for you to deal with this employee is to   8.____

   A. ask her to submit a written report to you on her complaint so that you can consider it fairly
   B. apologize for hurting her feelings and promise that she will be left alone in the future
   C. discuss her complaint with her, explaining again, and at greater length, the reason for your criticism
   D. ask her to apologize, since you would never allow yourself to be guilty of this kind of unfairness

9. Which of the following actions, if taken by an office supervisor, is MOST likely to lead to poor morale among his subordinates?
The supervisor

    A. promptly considers and tries to eliminate all rumors circulating in the office
    B. always uses his authority sparingly and without making an obvious display of it
    C. never makes personal issues out of matters that should be handled on an impersonal basis
    D. always applies the same disciplinary action for a certain infraction to every subordinate, no matter what his individual differences are

9.____

10. A certain operator under your supervision does very efficient work and is the most cooperative worker in the unit, but she usually reports to work late two or three times a week. For you, the supervisor, to ignore this worker's pattern of tardiness would be

    A. *good* because disciplining her in this matter may produce a negative effect on the worker's performance and cooperative spirit
    B. *good* because the worker may have personal reasons which prevent her from being on time for work every day
    C. *bad* because the personnel office will have increasing difficulty in keeping accurate time records for this worker if her lateness problem is not corrected
    D. *bad* because a supervisor is responsible for seeing that agency rules concerning required working hours are obeyed by all his subordinates

10.____

11. Suppose that you have to assign Operator A to do some extra work because Operator B has called in sick for the day.
In handling this situation, the action you, as the supervisor, should take FIRST is to

    A. explain to Operator A why there is extra work to do and why you are assigning it to her
    B. make a permanent record of Operator B's absence so that you can give her extra work to do when she comes back
    C. order Operator A to begin the work immediately and inform her that you will not tolerate any objections from her
    D. encourage Operator A to accept the job willingly by promising that Operator B will return the favor some day

11.____

12. Suppose that you, a newly appointed supervisor, are explaining a new procedure to several experienced operators in the unit. One of the operators tells you angrily that you really don't have any more experience than any other long-time operator and that any one of them could figure out the new procedure without being treated like new employees.
Of the following, what would be the BEST thing for you to tell this operator?

    A. Explain that, as a supervisor, you are automatically in a position to tell operators in your unit what do do.
    B. Explain that you do not mean to offend anyone, but that it is your responsibility as supervisor to make certain that the new procedure is clearly understood.
    C. Agree to let him figure out the procedure by himself, but warn him that he will be severely disciplined if he makes any mistakes.
    D. .Apologize for any unintended offense and agree that there is no need to continue your explanation since an experienced operator would be able to figure out the new procedure.

12.____

13. When training an employee in a fairly complicated new procedure, a supervisor should   13.__
generally use the four steps given below. These steps are in random order.
      I.   Demonstrate how to do the work.
      II.   Let the learner try the work himself.
      III.   Correct poor procedures by suggestion and demonstration.
      IV.   Explain the nature and purpose of the work.
The CORRECT order in which the supervisor should use these training steps is:

   A. IV, II, III, I   B. IV, I, II, III
   C. I, II, III, IV   D. II, III, I, IV

14. Suppose that you are supervising ten operators. You find that your fastest, most accurate   14.__
worker spends a great deal of time chatting with her co-workers, thereby keeping them
from finishing their work, although her own work is always finished with very few mistakes.
Of the following, the BEST thing for you to do is to

   A. discipline the operators who do not complete their work for talking on the job
   B. tell the talkative employee that her constant chatter is causing her own work to fall
down
   C. tell the employee that, while her own work is good, her chatting interferes with the
unit's work, and she must stop
   D. allow her to continue to talk to the other employees since this employee's own
good work makes up for anything else not completed

15. Suppose that you, a supervisor, find that one of the operators in your unit, who has the   15.__
potential to be a very good worker, has so little confidence in her own ability that it affects
her work.
The BEST thing for you to do is to

   A. tell the employee that her work is not good, but you know she is capable of much
better
   B. let the employee alone since the longer she works on the job, the more confidence
she will gain
   C. try to praise her work whenever possible and let her know you think she can be a
really good worker
   D. tell the other operators in the unit to try to build the employee's confidence in her
work

16. As a supervisor, you are training a new employee in various procedures. During your   16.__
explanation, the employee continually interrupts you with questions, some of which you
expect to cover later in your explanation.
Of the following, the BEST thing for you to do is to

   A. tell the employee to hold all her questions until you have finished your explanation
   B. answer the questions about things you had not planned to cover later, but tell the
employee to keep the other questions until you get to them
   C. answer the employee's questions as she asks them, and repeat the information
later in your explanation, if necessary
   D. let the employee know that she is making it difficult for you to explain the procedure
by asking so many questions

17. Good supervision is the starting place for an effective accident-prevention program. 17.____
In attempting to prevent accidents on the job, which of the following actions by a supervisor would be LEAST desirable? He

 A. observes the people he supervises to see that they are using the safe work practices he has trained them in
 B. makes sure that the people he supervises clearly understand the safety rules pertaining to their job
 C. acts as a model to the people he supervises by always following safe working practices in his own work
 D. stops the people he supervises from breaking safety rules only if he thinks an accident may happen

18. Assume that you supervise a unit of operators, each of whom has varying problems concerning the best way to do her work. Some operators demand your immediate and full attention when they have a problem; others require less supervision from you and try to be more independent in their work. 18.____
Of the following, the BEST way for you to stimulate a high level of work performance and morale in the group is to

 A. treat each member of your unit in exactly the same way to guarantee fair treatment
 B. deal with each member of your unit in terms of his or her needs and capacities
 C. give your attention only to important problems and ignore the operators who come to you with trivial ones
 D. take the approach that experienced operators should be able to solve their own problems

19. In which of the following circumstances would it be MOST appropriate for a supervisor to issue am order to his subordinates? 19.____

 A. When an important job is not finished by the end of the day, and someone is needed to work overtime
 B. When an unpleasant job has been given to the supervisor to assign to one of his staff members
 C. In an emergency situation involving the maintenance of physical safety of the staff members
 D. When a disciplinary problem arises with several employees who have previously always been cooperative and productive

20. Suppose that you, a supervisor of a large unit, find out that you have blamed and disciplined the wrong person for breaking an agency rule. 20.____
Of the following, the BEST action for you to take now is to

 A. frankly admit to this person that you had made a mistake and that you are sorry about it
 B. make no mention of your mistake, but lighten the workload of this person for a while to make up for it
 C. keep your error to yourself, but overlook the next mistake this person makes
 D. casually admit to your own supervisor that you made a judgment error and ask him not to reveal this mistake to the employee

21. A serious error has been discovered by a critical superior in work carried on under your supervision.
It is BEST to explain the situation and prevent its recurrence by

   A. claiming that you are not responsible because you do not check the work personally
   B. accepting the complaint and reporting the name of the employee responsible for the error
   C. informing him that such errors are bound to occur with a poorly trained staff and a heavy load of work
   D. assuring him that you will find out how it occurred so that you can have the work checked with greater care in the future

21.__

22. Suppose that the employees in your unit are required to perform a great deal of computation involving a large amount of addition and subtraction. Since accuracy is more important than speed in the work of your unit, employees are required to check all the figures used in the computations before turning in their work.
Of the following machines, the one which would be MOST practicable for the work of your unit is a

   A. listing adding machine
   B. comptometer
   C. punchcard tabulating machine
   D. billing machine

22.__

23. A supervisor is frequently required to prepare various types of written reports.
The one of the following features which is LEAST desirable in a lengthy report is that

   A. the style of writing should be readable, interesting, and impersonal; it should not be too scholarly, nor make use of involved sentence structure
   B. recommendations and conclusions resulting from the facts incorporated in the body of the report must appear only at the end of the report so that readers can follow the writer's line of reasoning
   C. in determining the extent of technical detail and terminology to be used in the presentation of supporting data, such as charts, tables, graphs, case examples, etc., the technical knowledge of the prospective reader or readers should be kept in mind
   D. the body of the report should mention all the pertinent facts and develop the writer's ideas in such a way that the recommendations will be a logical outgrowth of the arguments presented

23.__

24. The LEAST accurate of the following statements concerning the construction of an organization chart is that

   A. the relative positions of the boxes representing subdivisions in a line type organization should be determined by the hierarchical relationship of the subdivisions
   B. the main functions of subdivisions may be designed on the chart
   C. if the organization is complex, there may be a master chart and subsidiary charts
   D. the sizes of the boxes representing subdivisions of the organization should vary with the relative number of employees in the subdivisions

24.__

25. Instead of directing his attention solely toward devising new systems and procedures for 　　25.____
performing established clerical operations, the alert manager carefully studies these
operations with a view to determining the value that accrues to the organization from
their performance. Of the following, the MOST valid implication of this statement is that

   A. established clerical operations may not be of sufficient benefit to the organization
to justify their continuance
   B. devising new systems of performing clerical operations is no longer the function of
the office manager
   C. the performance of established clerical operations usually brings little or no direct
benefit to an organization
   D. devising better ways of performing a necessary clerical task may be of no value to
an organization

KEY (CORRECT ANSWERS)

1.	A	11.	A
2.	C	12.	B
3.	C	13.	B
4.	C	14.	C
5.	D	15.	C
6.	A	16.	C
7.	D	17.	D
8.	C	18.	B
9.	D	19.	C
10.	D	20.	A

21.	D
22.	A
23.	B
24.	D
25.	A

TEST 2

DIRECTIONS: Each question or incomplete statement is followed by several suggested answers or completions. Select the one that BEST answers the question or completes the statement. *PRINT THE LETTER OF THE CORRECT ANSWER IN THE SPACE AT THE RIGHT.*

1. For the supervisor of a computer installation, which of the following is LEAST likely to maintain effective control of operations?

    A. Perform each complex operation himself whenever possible
    B. See that each machine part is properly identified to avoid loss or misplacement
    C. Be sure (through a system of procedure control) that each job is effectively kept on the right track until it is finished
    D. Obtain factual data on operations actually performed in order to analyze machine, personnel, and job performance

1.____

2. Suppose that a probationary operator under your supervision refuses an assignment you have given him.
Your FIRST response to this situation should be to

    A. discuss with him his objections to the assignment
    B. order him to complete the assignment immediately
    C. make a note of the incident to build a case for firing him
    D. give him a more difficult task as punishment

2.____

3. Suppose that you have observed one of the operators under your supervision making offensive remarks about various minority groups to a co-worker. He has never made a statement like this to you nor offended any staff member. How would you handle this situation?

    A. Circulate a series of informationals regarding the existence of prejudice in an office setting
    B. Hold a staff meeting to discuss gossiping during office hours
    C. Discuss this matter with the operator involved, since his behavior is potentially harmful
    D. Report the matter to your supervisor so that he will take immediate action

3.____

4. One of the supervisor's primary functions is managing manpower and guiding it in the direction of attaining departmental objectives at maximum efficiency, with due regard for the individual personality differences of staff members.
Which of the following BEST describes what this paragraph implies about the supervisor's job? The supervisor('s)

    A. primarily stimulates action and follows up to see that staff members work efficiently towards departmental objectives
    B. responsibility is to promote good relations among the staff members and to get maximum work out of each staff member
    C. who manages and guides manpower efficiently wins and holds the respect of staff members
    D. awareness of the personality differences of staff members assures that work will be accomplished at maximum efficiency

4.____

5. Efficient production is the result of detail instruction. Which of the following is BEST   5.____
   deduced from this statement?

   A. Production and instruction are related.
   B. Lack of instruction reflects poor morale.
   C. Quality of instruction is dependent on production.
   D. Unsatisfactory production means poor instruction.

6. Assume that you are a supervisor in an agency which requires that you have periodic   6.____
   face-to-face discussions with each subordinate about his job performance. During such
   discussions, what is the MOST important objective you, as the supervisor, should keep in
   mind?

   A. Helping the employee to understand and improve his job performance
   B. Discussing the overall performance of the employee rather than a particular prob-
      lem
   C. The desirability of maintaining your popularity with your subordinates
   D. Warning the employee of possible disciplinary action where his performance does
      not meet acceptable standards

7. As a supervisor of operators, one of your responsibilities is the training of newly   7.____
   appointed operators.
   Of the following, which is the FIRST step that you should take with a new employee
   who has reported to you for the first time?

   A. Demonstrate exactly how the work is done
   B. Seat the new employee near an experienced worker
   C. Give an overall picture of the work done in the office
   D. Let the new employee do a job and then correct his mistakes

8. A supervisor has noticed that an operator in his unit, although usually punctual, is arriv-   8.____
   ing late for work frequently and looking tired all day. The supervisor has been told by
   another employee that the operator has an outside part-time job. His job performance
   remains satisfactory.
   Of the following, the BEST course of action for the supervisor to take is to

   A. warn the operator that continued lateness will result in his dismissal
   B. ask the head of data processing for instructions on how to proceed
   C. ignore the situation since the operator's job performance remains satisfactory
   D. talk to the operator privately about how to solve his lateness problem

9. Suppose that a new operator assigned to your unit has great difficulty learning his job   9.____
   despite the fact that you, as a supervisor, have spent several weeks trying to teach him.
   Of the following, which would be the MOST acceptable step to now take?

   A. Face the fact that the new employee is slow to learn and recommend dismissal
   B. Hold a private conference with the new employee and suggest that he try another
      type of work
   C. Reassess your training methods and try a new approach
   D. Stop trying to teach the work and let the new employee learn by himself through
      trial and error

10. Assume that you, a supervising operator, about to leave on vacation for two weeks, have been told that a number of important jobs must be completed by your unit before your return. During your absence, one of the senior operators under your supervision is to be designated to take your place.
Which of the following is it MOST important for you to do in turning over your work to the designated senior operator?

    A. Give the designated senior operator written, step-by-step instructions for the jobs to be completed during this two-week period and tell him to supervise the unit exactly as you had ,
    B. Tell the designated senior operator that you are delegating to him full responsibility for the successful completion of these jobs, and that he is to refer all other matters to your superior during your absence
    C. Give the designated senior operator sufficient instructions to enable him to complete these assignments, and advise both superiors and subordinates that he has been placed in charge of your unit
    D. Caution the designated senior operator about the necessity for avoiding mistakes in carrying out these assignments, since both of you will be blamed if anything goes wrong

10.__

11. You have been asked by the Chief of Data Processing to choose one of the operators under your supervision for a special assignment for a period of six months. It is a very desirable assignment which everyone in your unit wants, and you must decide upon the person who can do it best.
After you have made your decision, which of the following would be the BEST way in which to communicate it?

    A. Meet with your staff and tell them that you have chosen the worker in your unit who appears to be best fitted to the requirements for this assignment
    B. Speak to the operator you have chosen, instructing him not to tell anyone that he has been picked for this assignment
    C. Circulate a memo announcing the assignment to avoid questions from those not chosen
    D. Ask your own supervisor to make an announcement since he is less involved with the staff

11.__

12. Suppose that, as a supervising operator, you have received approval to change an important work process used in your unit. Some of the steps in the new process are the same as those in the old process. You have prepared written instructions for your subordinates.
For you also to hold a staff meeting to instruct your subordinates on the changes would be

    A. *unnecessary* since the written instructions are available to employees
    B. *desirable* because this meeting would avoid the necessity of detailed written instructions
    C. *undesirable* since some subordinates always object to changes and encourage resistance at meetings
    D. *desirable* since the meeting, together with written instructions, can help to clarify questions

12.__

13. A new operator has been assigned to your unit. After two months, you find that he still makes many errors in his work and has a negative attitude about the job. You do not consider him a positive addition to your staff.
What should you do FIRST in resolving this situation?

    A. Tell the new operator he will be fired if his work does not improve
    B. Before his negative attitude affects others, recommend his dismissal
    C. Recommend that the new operator be transferred to another unit for further evaluation
    D. Attempt to determine the reasons for the new operator's errors and poor attitude

13.____

Questions 14-17.

DIRECTIONS: Questions 14 through 17 are to be answered SOLELY on the basis of the information given in the following paragraph.

The first requirement for developing delegation of authority is to realize the need for it. A supervisor must recognize that as long as he is limited to doing what he can accomplish himself, he will always be short of time and limited in his achievements. The alternative is to acquire aides, train them, and permit them to do the job, even if their manner of doing it differs from how the supervisor might have done it. Competent aides are mandatory for group efforts to reach greatest heights. A supervisor needs to multiply himself. It is nonsense to try to lead the band and play all the instruments too. For delegation to work effectively, certain criteria can assist materially. Important is the establishment of definite goals and clear policies, for these give guidance to the subordinate and keep him from going too far astray in the fulfillment of the tasks. Work which is routine and which is covered by definite policies should offer little delegation difficulty. Clear and timely communication, complete instructions and orders, definite job identifications, and the use of broad controls expedite delegation, for they all can help supply the desired checks to determine whether the work is being accomplished satisfactorily.

14. The one of the following which is the MOST suitable title for the above paragraph is

    A. CONVINCING SUBORDINATES TO ACCEPT AUTHORITY
    B. THE ACQUISITION OF AIDES
    C. COMMUNICATIONS IN PUBLIC AGENCIES
    D. DEVELOPING DELEGATION OF AUTHORITY

14.____

15. The phrase *to try to lead the band and play all the instruments too* is a reference to

    A. a supervisor trying to do all the work himself despite having subordinates
    B. a supervisor trying to be a leader and a follower at the same time
    C. trying to supervise a department and simultaneously maintaining outside interests
    D. the fact that band leaders make poor supervisors

15.____

16. According to the above paragraph, in order to keep his subordinates from going too far astray in the fulfillment of their assigned tasks, the supervisor should

    A. schedule daily conferences with them
    B. teach them to do their assigned tasks exactly as he would
    C. establish definite goals and clear policies
    D. assign to them only work which is routine

16.____

17. According to the above paragraph, the use of clear and timely communication helps to expedite delegation since it can help

    A. make the supervisor clarify policy changes as soon as they are issued
    B. the supervisor acquire aides whom he can train
    C. create the desired checks to find out whether the work is being done satisfactorily
    D. establish definite job identifications

17.___

Questions 18-21.

DIRECTIONS: Questions 18 through 21 are to be answered SOLELY on the basis of the information given in the following passage.

The supervisor is the key man in any safety program. To the worker, he is management. Most of the thoughts and plans of executives must sift through to the workers by way of their supervisors. Safety is directly related to each employee's temperament, his attitude toward his work and management, his ideas of obedience and his sense of responsibility, and even to his idea of fun.

The supervisor is indispensable to good safety work, for he is the immediate contact for and the immediate control of the workers. It is seldom feasible or advisable to hire supervisors solely on the basis of their attitudes toward safety, consequently, the problem is one of enlisting the supervisors' interest in safety. Few better methods for creating such interest among supervisors can be found than that of identifying safety with efficiency and production. That accident losses hurt the showing of the department and of the supervisor should be made clear to him.

18. According to the above passage, there is a DIRECT relationship between safety and the

    A. flow of communication among executives
    B. exchange of ideas on safety between first-line supervisors
    C. amount of safety literature distributed to employees
    D. workers' attitudes toward their supervisors

18.___

19. It may be MOST reasonably concluded from the discussion on the supervisor's role in safety programs that the supervisor should be

    A. hired on the basis of his attitudes toward safety
    B. expected to attend courses on safety methods
    C. encouraged to become interested in safety
    D. made interested in safety programs primarily through group discussion techniques

19.___

20. According to the above passage, equating safety with efficiency and production is one of the BEST ways to cause

    A. a supervisor to become interested in safety
    B. the workers to lose interest in their jobs
    C. the executives to be more secretive in their plans
    D. the hiring only of supervisors who assign the highest priority to safety

20.___

21. Of the following, the MOST suitable title for the above passage is   21.____

    A. RECRUITING SUPERVISORS TO CREATE SAFETY PROGRAMS
    B. HOW WORKER ATTITUDES AFFECT SAFETY
    C. HOW ACCIDENT LOSSES AFFECT PRODUCTION
    D. SAFETY AND THE SUPERVISOR

Questions 22-25.

DIRECTIONS: Questions 22 through 25 are to be answered SOLELY on the basis of the infor-
              mation given in the following passage.

*The supervisor plays an important role in a work-standards program. In many cases, he
must set the standards, install them, and see that they are applied. In large departments,
analysts may be brought in from the outside to set work standards, but, even then, the supervisor plays a leading role through his work with the analyst and his task of cheeking employee
performance against standards.*

*The concept of work standards should not be difficult for supervisors to absorb. They
must employ it in carrying out nearly all their responsibilities. For example, they must evaluate prospective employees in terms of a standard. In carrying out their work improvement
responsibilities, supervisors are expected to train workers in order to bring them to a level of
competent, satisfactory performance. When evaluating employees and recommending promotions, transfers, and dismissals, supervisors compare employee performance to a work
standard. Similarly, the work standards concept is essential to the supervisor if he is to recognize and maintain a satisfactory level of employee production.*

22. Of the following, the BEST title for the above passage is   22.____

    A. HOW TO SET WORK STANDARDS
    B. THE IMPORTANCE OF WORK STANDARDS TO A SUPERVISOR
    C. EMPLOYING AN OUTSIDE WORK-STANDARDS ANALYST
    D. A SUPERVISOR'S RESPONSIBILITIES

23. According to the above passage, when are outside analysts brought in?   23.____
    To

    A. judge the supervisor's work
    B. decide which employees should be dismissed
    C. check employee performance
    D. set work standards

24. The above passage discusses several ways in which a supervisor's work involves the   24.____
    concept of work standards. Which of the following is NOT discussed as one of these
    ways?

    A. The supervisor designing standards himself
    B. An outside analyst working with a supervisor
    C. Joint development of complex standards
    D. Comparing performance against standards

25. The above passage indicates that work standards are 25.____
    A. rarely used by supervisors
    B. disliked by most employees
    C. used for the purpose of keeping employee production at an adequate level
    D. used for the purpose of evaluating an outside analyst

———

KEY (CORRECT ANSWERS)

1.	A		11.	A
2.	A		12.	D
3.	C		13.	D
4.	A		14.	D
5.	A		15.	A
6.	A		16.	C
7.	C		17.	C
8.	D		18.	D
9.	C		19.	C
10.	C		20.	A

21.	D
22.	A
23.	C
24.	A
25.	A

———

EXAMINATION SECTION
TEST 1

DIRECTIONS: Each question or incomplete statement is followed by several suggested answers or completions. Select the one that BEST answers the question or completes the statement. *PRINT THE LETTER OF THE CORRECT ANSWER IN THE SPACE AT THE RIGHT.*

1. A certain supervisor must periodically schedule the work for her unit's operators. Of the following, the LEAST significant factor for her to consider when scheduling the work is
    A. hardware problems
    B. increases or decreases in volume of work
    C. repeated inquiries from non-priority users
    D. the operators' leave schedules

    1.____

2. Assume that you are in charge of a small unit and have just received a new, complex job. Of the following, the BEST way for you to insure the proper completion of the job is to
    A. assume that experience gained on other jobs will enable your operators to do this job without any difficulty
    B. prepare a written layout and instructions for the new jobs and distribute them to your operators
    C. speak to each operator individually and explain the new job
    D. speak to the entire unit at one time and explain the new job to them as a group

    2.____

3. Suppose that a new and inexperienced operator is assigned to you for training. You observe that she is very nervous and tense. Of the following, the BEST way for you to begin training her is to
    A. assure her that nobody has ever had any trouble following your instructions and so you are sure that she will do very well
    B. assure her that there is no need for her to feel nervous because the job is very easy and almost anyone can do it without any trouble
    C. tell her that you can understand how she might feel nervous and that you will do all you can to help her adjust
    D. tell her that she does not have to feel nervous because the agency's production standards are quite low

    3.____

4.   A supervisor generally has the authority to tell subordinates what work they should do, how they should do it, and when it should be done. Of the following, the MOST important reason for a supervisor to have this authority is that usually

    A. work is accomplished more effectively if the supervisor plans and coordinates it

    B. most people will not work unless there is someone with authority standing over them

    C. supervisor must have complete control over their subordinates' behavior in order for a unit to function properly

    D. subordinates are not familiar with the tasks to be performed

4._____

5.   In which of the following situations is it MOST appropriate for a supervisor to issue a direct order? When

    A. a subordinate makes a mistake on a piece of work and the worker should have known better because he performed the task well many times before

    B. the safety of a co-worker is involved

    C. the supervisor has to give an unpleasant assignment to a subordinate who will probably not want to take on the job

    D. a co-worker questions the soundness of an agency directive

5._____

6.   One of the operators whom you supervise asks your opinion about some unclear information on a source document sent to you by another office. You look at the document and are not certain what the information is. Of the following, the BEST procedure for you to follow is to

    A. return the document to the other office with a note indicating that the information cannot be entered because it is unclear

    B. see whether there is another document from that office containing similar information which you can use

    C. telephone the other office and ask someone for the information which is not clear

    D. tell the operator to enter as much of the information as is possible and to omit the unclear information

6._____

7.   Supposes that you, the supervisor of a unit, finds that one of your best operators is talking too much with the other operators and not getting her work done. In this situation, the FIRST of the following steps that you should take is to

    A. review with her the pertinent rules and regulations of the office and tell her that she is expected to follow them

    B. indicate to her the changes you have observed in her behavior and ask if she has a problem that she might want to discuss with you

    C. tell her that you are very disappointed in her because she is not working in her usual manner and that if she does not improve immediately you will have to take disciplinary action

    D. tell her that if her recent behavior continues you will have to give her a negative evaluation

7._____

8. A good supervisor knows that motivation of a subordinate is important if
successful training is to take place. Of the following, which is generally NOT an
example of good motivation? The supervisor

    A. explains to the worker how the worker may have fewer problems on the
job if he gets the training

    B. tells the worker how the training will help the subordinate work more
efficiently

    C. explains to the worker how the training may lead to a promotion

    D. tells the worker that successful completion of the training is essential for
the worker to maintain his position

8.____

9. Assume that one of the operators whom you supervise suggests what you
believe to be a useful change in the way in which certain operations are
performed in your unit. Of the following steps that you might take, it is MOST
important that you make sure that

    A. the employee receives complete credit for having made the suggestion

    B. the employee is not aware of any improvements you make in the
suggestion before you submit it to your supervisor

    C. you thank the employee and remind him that he is expected to make
useful suggestions from time to time

    D. you review the suggestion carefully and then present it as an idea you
both worked on

9.____

10. Of the following reasons, the MAIN reason that a supervisor should investigate
the causes of an accident is so the supervisor can

    A. take whatever steps may be necessary to prevent a similar accident from
happening again

    B. properly punish the individual responsible for the accident

    C. discover whether the agency is liable for any injuries sustained

    D. have a suitable example to use during the next discussion of office safety
practices

10.____

11. Assume that one of the operators in your unit does not complete an assignment
properly because she fails to follow the instructions you gave her. Of the
following, the FIRST action you should take when you discover what has
happened is to

    A. ask her to do the job again correctly

    B. find out whether the operator understood your instructions

    C. review the operator's previous performance to see if similar incidents
have occurred in the past

    D. tell the operator that she should listen more carefully the next time you
give her instructions

11.____

12. One of your operators asks you a question about the proper procedure to use   12.____
for a job she is working on. You are not sure of the correct answer. Of the
following, the FIRST action which you should take is to
   A. ask the operator to find out whether any of her co-workers can answer
      her question
   B. suggest to the operator that she speak with your supervisor and report
      back to you any information she receives
   C. tell the operator that you are not certain of the answer and that you will try
      to get the information
   D. tell the operator to follow whatever procedure she has used for similar
      jobs

13. Assume that one of your usually reliable operators has told you that a job   13.____
had been verified. After the job was forwarded to the user, you are informed
that the job was not verified. Of the following, the BEST approach for you to
use when discussing this matter with the operator is to
   A. apologize to the operator for having to discuss the matter, state your
      criticism, and try to balance it with an indication that the error was an easy
      one to make
   B. avoid making a personal attack on the operator, state your criticism, and
      try to balance it with praise for good work she has done
   C. be firm with the operator, state your criticism, and indicate that you will be
      watching her work closely in the future
   D. speak with the operator about an unrelated matter, then casually mention
      your criticism, and tell her that this is just a minor point and not something
      that she should worry about

14. One afternoon you notice that one of your operators has made the same   14.____
mistake on several jobs which she did in the morning. In the past, the operator
has not made this kind of mistake. Of the following, the BEST course of action
for you to take to avoid a repetition of this mistake is to
   A. correct the mistakes yourself and say nothing to the operator since you
      are aware that she knows the proper way of doing the work
   B. correct the mistakes yourself and then tell the operator that you realize
      she knows how to do the work properly
   C. tell the operator that you have discovered the mistakes and give her a
      short review on how to do this phase of the job
   D. use the opportunity to retrain the operator in all phases of the job so that
      she will not make mistakes in the future

15. Assume that you are supervising a unit of five operators. Your supervisor has   15.____
give you a standardized set of instructions for abbreviating mailing addresses
which your operators are to follow. After you have trained them in the use of
this standard abbreviation procedure, you check several mailing jobs and find
that two of the operators are not following these instructions. Of the following,
the BEST action for you to take is to
   A. call a meeting with your five operators so that you can review with them
      the proper method for doing the job

B. distribute the incorrectly done jobs to the other operators to be done in accordance with your instructions
C. point out to the two operators that the job must be done according to the instructions you gave them and have them redo the job
D. ask the two operators why they did the job as they did and then decide for yourself whether the job is acceptable as it is

16. A supervisor notices that one of the operators whom she supervises is having difficulty concentrating on her assignments. The operator often seems nervous and tense, and is making many more errors in her work than she had made in the past. Which of the following is the BEST action for the supervisor to take in this situation?   16._____
    A. Begin to keep a written record of the mistakes the operator is making so that the supervisor can show it to her at a disciplinary interview
    B. Suggest to the operator that she needs medical attention or counseling to help her with whatever problem she has
    C. Tell the operator that she is expected to keep her production up to the level she had maintained in the past
    D. Try to find out why the operator is having difficulties with her tasks and then try to help her

17. After you have criticized the poor work of one of your operators, the operator tells you that she feels you are picking on her. Of the following, the MOST appropriate course of action for you to take is to   17._____
    A. ignore her statement since most people just cannot accept criticism
    B. tell her that she should take her complaint to your supervisor if she feels that you have unfairly criticized her
    C. explain your criticism in detail and inform her that you are trying to help her do a better job
    D. apologize to her but inform her that you will watch her work even more closely in the future

18. You observe that one of your operators consistently finishes her work before any other operator in your unit. All your operators are assigned the same workload. After you have made sure that her work is accurate, the MOST appropriate action for you to take is to   18._____
    A. ask her to train the other operators to work as rapidly as she does
    B. ask her whether she has any special methods which she uses to complete the work so quickly
    C. give her a greater amount of work to do than you give the other operators
    D. indicate her speed to the other operators and ask them why they cannot work as quickly

19. Assume that you are assigned as supervisor in charge of the night shift. Your instructions are that all work is to be verified by your unit's verifier. When you begin to assign the work one night, you discover that the day shift supervisor has not left any indication of which jobs have been verified. Of the following, the BEST action for you to take in this situation is to   19._____
    A. verify all jobs by the day shift so as not to have any unverified work

B. call the day shift supervisor at home and find out which jobs were verified

C. set aside the jobs done by the day shift to ensure that the verifying will not be done twice

D. verify only those jobs without a notch along the right-hand edge

20. Suppose that you are given a new procedure for your unit to implement immediately. You explain the new procedure to the operators under your supervision and some of them complain that the new procedure is not as good as the one they have been following. Of the following, the BEST way to handle these complaints is to
    20.____
    A. answer the operators' complaints as best you can and then request the operators' cooperation in following the new procedure
    B. let the operators follow the old procedure and tell them you will present their complaints to your supervisor
    C. tell the operators that you are their supervisor and they must follow your instructions
    D. tell the operators that though you agree with their complaints, a management decision should not be questioned

21. Suppose that one of your operators has fallen far behind in his work and complains to you that he has more work than any of the other operators. You know, however, that you distribute the work equally among the operators. Which one of the following actions is the MOST appropriate for you to take FIRST in this situation?
    21.____
    A. Check the operator's personnel records to see what kind of performance ratings he was given previously.
    B. Distribute some of his work to the other operators until he is able to bring his work up to date.
    C. Observe the operator while he performs his job to see whether his work methods are correct.
    D. Tell one of the other operators to observe him and suggest ways to help him catch up with his work.

22. Assume that you have to instruct an operator in a new and involved procedure. Of the following, the BEST sequence to follow when instructing the operator in this procedure is:
    22.____
    A. I. Demonstrate for the operator how the work is done.
       II. Let the operator try it.
       III. Explain the nature and purpose of the work.
       IV. Correct errors by suggestion and demonstration.
    B. I. Explain the nature and purpose of the work.
       II. Let the operator try it himself.
       III. Demonstrate how it should be done.
       IV. Correct errors by suggestion and demonstration.
    C. I. Explain the nature and purpose of the work.
       II. Demonstrate how it is done.
       III. Let the operator try it himself.
       IV. Correct errors by suggestion and demonstration.

D. I. Let the operator try the work himself
   II. Demonstrate how he should do it.
   III. Correct errors by suggestion and demonstration.
   IV. Explain the nature and purpose of the work.

23. After having initially trained workers of a user section in their new job tasks,   23.____
    it is BEST for you as a trainer to
    A. turn the group over completely to their regular supervisor for any further
       training
    B. follow up very closely to see that they are doing the work properly
    C. restrict any further contact with the group to those workers who seem
       to have the most difficulty
    D. begin your training role but make yourself unavailable as a consultant

24. In the course of instructing a trainee in the operation of a machine, there   24.____
    comes a time when it is best to let the trainee make an initial trial under
    the instructor's direct supervision. This step in the learning sequence is usually
    IMMEDIATELY _____ of the machine.
    A. *before* the instructor demonstrates the operation
    B. *before* the instructor explains the purpose
    C. *after* the instructor demonstrates the operation
    D. *after* the instructor explains the purpose

25. As a supervisor, you have received a rather complicated set of instructions   25.____
    for a new project which is to begin immediately. Some of the instructions are
    confusing. Your FIRST step should be to
    A. attempt to clear up with your supervisor any ambiguities before beginning
       the project
    B. instruct your staff to get started on the project immediately while you try to
       clarify the instructions
    C. discuss the matter with other supervisors at your level to find out if they
       have received clarification
    D. figure out the instructions as best you can and provide firm guidelines for
       your subordinates on the basis of your own good judgment

---

KEY (CORRECT ANSWERS)

1.	C		11.	B
2.	B		12.	C
3.	C		13.	B
4.	A		14.	C
5.	B		15.	C
6.	C		16.	D
7.	A		17.	C
8.	D		18.	B
9.	A		19.	D
10.	A		20.	C

21.	C
22.	C
23.	B
24.	C
25.	A

EXAMINATION SECTION
TEST 1

DIRECTIONS: Each question or incomplete statement is followed by several suggested answers or completions. Select the one that BEST answers the question or completes the statement. *PRINT THE LETTER OF THE CORRECT ANSWER IN THE SPACE AT THE RIGHT.*

1. In public agencies, communications should be based PRIMARILY on a
   A. two-way flow from the top down and from the bottom up, most of which should be given in writing to avoid ambiguity
   B. multi-direction flow among all levels and with outside persons
   C. rapid, internal one-way flow from the top down
   D. two-way flow of information, most of which should be given orally for purposes of clarity

   1.____

2. In some organizations, changes in policy or procedures are often communicated by word of mouth from supervisors to employees with no prior discussion or exchange of viewpoints with employees.
   This procedure often produces employee dissatisfaction CHIEFLY because
   A. information is mostly unusable since a considerable amount of time is required to transmit information
   B. lower-level supervisors tend to be excessively concerned with minor details
   C. management has failed to seek employees' advice before making changes
   D. valuable staff time is lost between decision-making and the implementation of decisions

   2.____

3. For good letter writing, you should try to visualize the person to whom you are writing, especially if you know him.
   Of the following rules, it is LEAST helpful in such visualization to think of
   A. the person's likes and dislikes, his concerns, and his needs
   B. what you would be likely to say if speaking in person
   C. what you would expect to be asked if speaking in person
   D. your official position in order to be certain that your words are proper

   3.____

4. One approach to good informal letter writing is to make letters and conversational.
   All of the following practices will usually help to do this EXCEPT:
   A. If possible, use a style which is similar to the style used when speaking
   B. Substitute phrases for single words (e.g., *at the present time* for *now*)
   C. Use contractions of words (e.g., *you're* for *you are*)
   D. Use ordinary vocabulary when possible

   4.____

5. All of the following rules will aid in producing clarity in report-writing EXCEPT: 5.____
   A. Give specific details or examples, if possible
   B. Keep related words close together in each sentence
   C. Present information in sequential order
   D. Put several thoughts or ideas in each paragraph

6. The one of the following statements about public relations which is MOST 6.____
   accurate is that
   A. in the long run, appearance gains better results than performance
   B. objectivity is decreased if outside public relations consultants are
      employed
   C. public relations is the responsibility of every employee
   D. public relations should be based on a formal publicity program

7. The form of communication which is usually considered to be MOST personally 7.____
   directed to the intended recipient is the
   A. brochure   B. film   C. letter   D. radio

8. In general, a document that presents an organization's views or opinions 8.____
   on a particular topic is MOST accurately known as a
   A. tear sheet   B. position paper
   C. flyer   D. journal

9. Assume that you have been asked to speak before an organization of persons 9.____
   who oppose a newly announced program in which you are involved. You feel
   tense about talking to this group.
   Which of the following rules generally would be MOST useful in gaining rapport
   when speaking before the audience?
   A. Impress them with your experience
   B. Stress all areas of disagreement
   C. Talk to the group as to one person
   D. Use formal grammar and language

10. An organization must have an effective public relations program since, at its 10.____
    best, public relations is a bridge to change.
    All of the following statements about communication and human behavior have
    validity EXCEPT:
    A. People are more likely to talk about controversial matters with like-minded
       people than with those holding other views
    B. The earlier an experience, the more powerful its effect since it influences
       how later experiences will be interpreted
    C. In periods of social tension, official sources gain increased believability
    D. Those who are already interested in a topic are the ones who are most
       open to receive new communications about it

11. An employee should be encouraged to talk easily and frankly when he is dealing with his supervisor.
In order to encourage such free communication, it would be MOST appropriate for a supervisor to behave in a(n)
    A. sincere manner; assure the employee that you will deal with him honestly and openly
    B. official manner; you are a supervisor and must always act formally with subordinates
    C. investigative manner; you must probe and question to get to a basis of trust
    D. unemotional manner; the employee's emotions and background should play no part in your dealings with him

11.____

12. Research findings show that an increase in free communication within an agency GENERALLY results in which one of the following?
    A. Improved morale and productivity
    B. Increased promotional opportunities
    C. An increase in authority
    D. A spirit of honesty

12.____

13. Assume that you are a supervisor and your superiors have given you a new-type procedure to be followed.
Before passing this information on to your subordinates, the one of the following actions that you should take FIRST is to
    A. ask your superiors to send out a memorandum to the entire staff
    B. clarify the procedure in your own mind
    C. set up a training course to provide instruction on the new procedure
    D. write a memorandum to your subordinates

13.____

14. Communication is necessary for an organization to be effective.
The one of the following which is LEAST important for most communication systems is that
    A. messages are sent quickly and directly to the person who needs them to operate
    B. information should be conveyed understandably and accurately
    C. the method used to transmit information should be kept secret so that security can be maintained
    D. senders of messages must know how their messages are received and acted upon

14.____

15. Which one of the following is the CHIEF advantage of listening willingly to subordinates and encouraging them to talk freely and honestly?
It
    A. reveals to supervisors the degree to which ideas that are passed down are accepted by subordinates
    B. reduces the participation of subordinates in the operation of the department
    C. encourages subordinates to try for promotion
    D. enables supervisors to learn more readily what the *grapevine* is saying

15.____

16. A supervisor may be informed through either oral or written reports.   16._____
Which one of the following is an ADVANTAGE of using oral reports?
   A. There is no need for a formal record of the report.
   B. An exact duplicate of the report is not easily transmitted to others.
   C. A good oral report requires little time for preparation.
   D. An oral report involves two-way communication between a subordinate and his supervisor.

17. Of the following, the MOST important reason why supervisors should   17._____
communicate effectively with the public is to
   A. improve the public's understanding of information that is important for them to know
   B. establish a friendly relationship
   C. obtain information about the kinds of people who come to the agency
   D. convince the public that services are adequate

18. Supervisors should generally NOT use phrases like *too hard*, *too easy*, and   18._____
a lot PRINCIPALLY because such phrases
   A. may be offensive to some minority groups
   B. are too informal
   C. mean different things to different people
   D. are difficult to remember

19. The ability to communicate clearly and concisely is an important element in   19._____
effective leadership.
Which of the following statements about oral and written communication is
GENERALLY true?
   A. Oral communication is more time-consuming.
   B. Written communication is more likely to be misinterpreted.
   C. Oral communication is useful only in emergencies.
   D. Written communication is useful mainly when giving information to fewer than twenty people.

20. Rumors can often have harmful and disruptive effects on an organization.   20._____
Which one of the following is the BEST way to prevent rumors from becoming a
problem?
   A. Refuse to act on rumors, thereby making them less believable.
   B. Increase the amount of information passed along by the *grapevine*.
   C. Distribute as much factual information as possible.
   D. Provide training in report writing.

21. Suppose that a subordinate asks you about a rumor he has heard. The rumor   21._____
deals with a subject which your superiors consider *confidential*.
Which of the following BEST describes how you should answer the
subordinate? Tell

A. the subordinate that you don't make the rules and that he should speak to higher ranking officials
B. the subordinate that you will ask your superior for information
C. him only that you cannot comment on the matter
D. him the rumor is not true

22. Supervisors often find it difficult to *get their message across* when instructing newly appointed employees in their various duties.
The MAIN reason for this is generally that the
A. duties of the employees have increased
B. supervisor is often so expert in his area that he fails to see it from the learner's point of view
C. supervisor adapts his instruction to the slowest learner in the group
D. new employees are younger, less concerned with job security and more interested in fringe benefits

22.____

23. Assume that you are discussing a job problem with an employee under your supervision. During the discussion, you see that the man's eyes are turning away from you and that he is not paying attention.
In order to get the man's attention, you should FIRST
A. ask him to look you in the eye   B. talk to him about sports
C. tell him he is being very rude   D. change your tone of voice

23.____

24. As a supervisor, you may find it necessary to conduct meetings with your subordinates.
Of the following, which would be MOST helpful in assuring that a meeting accomplishes the purpose for which it was called?
A. Give notice of the conclusions you would like to reach at the start of the meeting.
B. Delay the start of the meeting until everyone is present.
C. Write down points to be discussed in proper sequence.
D. Make sure everyone is clear on whatever conclusions have been reached and on what must be done after the meeting.

24.____

25. Every supervisor will occasionally be called upon to deliver a reprimand to a subordinate. If done properly, this can greatly help an employee improve his performance.
Which one of the following is NOT a good practice to follow when giving a reprimand?
A. Maintain your composure and temper
B. Reprimand a subordinate in the presence of other employees so they can learn the same lesson
C. Try to understand why the employee was not able to perform satisfactorily
D. Let your knowledge of the man involved determine the exact nature of the reprimand

25.____

KEY (CORRECT ANSWERS)

1.	C		11.	A
2.	B		12.	A
3.	D		13.	B
4.	B		14.	C
5.	D		15.	A
6.	C		16.	D
7.	C		17.	A
8.	B		18.	C
9.	C		19.	B
10.	C		20.	C

21.	B
22.	B
23.	D
24.	D
25.	B

————

TEST 2

DIRECTIONS: Each question or incomplete statement is followed by several suggested answers or completions. Select the one that BEST answers the question or completes the statement. *PRINT THE LETTER OF THE CORRECT ANSWER IN THE SPACE AT THE RIGHT.*

1. Usually one thinks of communication as a single step, essentially that of transmitting an idea.
   Actually, however, this is only part of a total process, the FIRST step of which should be
   A. the prompt dissemination of the idea to those who may be affected by it
   B. motivating those affected to take the required action
   C. clarifying the idea in one's own mind
   D. deciding to whom the idea is to be communicated

   1.____

2. Research studies on patterns of informal communication have concluded that most individuals in a group tend to be passive recipients of news, while a few make it their business to spread it around in an organization.
   With this conclusion in mind, it would be MOST correct for the supervisor to attempt to identify these few individuals and
   A. give them the complete facts on important matters in advance of others
   B. inform the other subordinates of the identity of these few individuals so that their influence may be minimized
   C. keep them straight on the facts on important matters
   D. warn them to cease passing along any information to others

   2.____

3. The one of the following which is the PRINCIPAL advantage of making an oral report is that it
   A. affords an immediate opportunity for two-way communication between the subordinate and superior
   B. is an easy method for the superior to use in transmitting information to others of equal rank
   C. saves the time of all concerned
   D. permits more precise pinpointing of praise or blame by means of follow-up questions by the superior

   3.____

4. An agency may sometimes undertake a public relations program of a defensive nature.
   With reference to the use of defensive public relations, it would be MOST correct to state that it
   A. is bound to be ineffective since defensive statements, even though supported by factual data, can never hope to even partly overcome the effects of prior unfavorable attacks
   B. proves that the agency has failed to establish good relationships with newspapers, radio stations, or other means of publicity

   4.____

C. shows that the upper echelons of the agency have failed to develop sound public relations procedures and techniques

D. is sometimes required to aid morale by protecting the agency from unjustified criticism and misunderstanding of policies or procedures

5. Of the following factors which contribute to possible undesirable public attitudes towards an agency, the one which is MOST susceptible to being changed by the efforts of the individual employee in an organization is that   5._____
   A. enforcement of unpopular regulations as offended many individuals
   B. the organization itself has an unsatisfactory reputation
   C. the public is not interested in agency matters
   D. there are many errors in judgment committed by individual subordinates

6. It is not enough for an agency's services to be of a high quality; attention must also be given to the acceptability of these services to the general public.
This statement is GENERALLY   6._____
   A. *false*; a superior quality of service automatically wins public support
   B. *true*; the agency cannot generally progress beyond the understanding and support of the public
   C. *false*; the acceptance by the public of agency services determines their quality
   D. *true*; the agency is generally unable to engage in any effective enforcement activity without public support

7. Sustained agency participation in a program sponsored by a community organization is MOST justified when   7._____
   A. the achievement of agency objectives in some area depends partly on the activity of this organization
   B. the community organization is attempting to widen the base of participation in all community affairs
   C. the agency is uncertain as to what the community wants
   D. the agency is uncertain as to what the community wants

8. Of the following, the LEAST likely way in which a records system may serve a supervisor is in   8._____
   A. developing a sympathetic and cooperative public attitude toward the agency
   B. improving the quality of supervision by permitting a check on the accomplishment of subordinates
   C. permit a precise prediction of the exact incidences in specific categories for the following year
   D. helping to take the guesswork out of the distribution of the agency

9. Assuming that the *grapevine* in any organization is virtually indestructible, the one of the following which it is MOST important for management to understand is:
    A. What is being spread by means of the *grapevine* and the reason for spreading it
    B. What is being spread by means of the *grapevine* and how it is being spread
    C. Who is involved in spreading the information that is on the *grapevine*
    D. Why those who are involved in spreading the information are doing so

9.____

10. When the supervisor writes a report concerning an investigation to which he has been assigned, it should be LEAST intended to provide
    A. a permanent official record of relevant information gathered
    B. a summary of case findings limited to facts which tend to indicate the guilt of a suspect
    C. a statement of the facts on which higher authorities may base a corrective or disciplinary action
    D. other investigators with information so that they may continue with other phases of the investigation

10.____

11. In survey work, questionnaires rather than interviews are sometimes used. The one of the following which is a DISADVANTAGE of the questionnaire method as compared with the interview is the
    A. difficulty of accurately interpreting the results
    B. problem of maintaining anonymity of the participant
    C. fact that it is relatively uneconomical
    D. requirement of special training for the distribution of questionnaires

11.____

12. in his contacts with the public, an employee should attempt to create a good climate of support for his agency.
    This statement is GENERALLY
    A. *false*; such attempts are clearly beyond the scope of his responsibility
    B. *true*; employees of an agency who come in contact with the public have the opportunity to affect public relations
    C. *false*; such activity should be restricted to supervisors trained in public relations techniques
    D. *true*; the future expansion of the agency depends to a great extent on continued public support of the agency

12.____

13. The repeated use by a supervisor of a call for volunteers to get a job done is objectionable MAINLY because it
    A. may create a feeling of animosity between the volunteers and the non-volunteers
    B. may indicate that the supervisor is avoiding responsibility for making assignments which will be most productive
    C. is an indication that the supervisor is not familiar with the individual capabilities of his men
    D. is unfair to men who, for valid reasons, do not, or cannot volunteer

13.____

14. Of the following statements concerning subordinates' expressions to a
supervisor of their opinions and feelings concerning work situations, the one
which is MOST correct is that
    A. by listening and responding to such expressions the supervisor
encourages the development of complaints
    B. the lack of such expressions should indicate to the supervisor that there is
a high level of job satisfaction
    C. the more the supervisor listens to and responds to such expressions, the
more he demonstrates lack of supervisory ability
    D. by listening and responding to such expressions, the supervisor will
enable many subordinates to understand and solve their own problems
on the job

14.____

15. In attempting to motivate employees, rewards are considered preferable to
punishment PRIMARILY because
    A. punishment seldom has any effect on human behavior
    B. punishment usually results in decreased production
    C. supervisors find it difficult to punish
    D. rewards are more likely to result in willing cooperation

15.____

16. In an attempt to combat the low morale in his organization, a high level
supervisor publicized an *open-door policy* to allow employees who wished to
do so to come to him with their complaints.
Which of the following is LEAST likely to account for the fact that no employee
came in with a complaint?
    A. Employees are generally reluctant to go over the heads of their
immediate supervisor.
    B. The employees did not feel that management would help them.
    C. The low morale was not due to complaints associated with the job.
    D. The employees felt that they had more to lose than to gain.

16.____

17. It is MOST desirable to use written instructions rather than oral instructions for
a particular job when
    A. a mistake on the job will not be serious
    B. the job can be completed in a short time
    C. there is no need to explain the job minutely
    D. the job involves many details

17.____

18. If you receive a telephone call regarding a matter which your office does not
handle, you should FIRST
    A. give the caller the telephone number of the proper office so that he can
dial again
    B. offer to transfer the caller to the proper office
    C. suggest that the caller re-dial since he probably dialed incorrectly
    D. tell the caller he has reached the wrong office and then hang up

18.____

19. When you answer the telephone, the MOST important reason for identifying   19.____
yourself and your organization is to
    A. give the caller time to collect his or her thoughts
    B. impress the caller with your courtesy
    C. inform the caller that he or she has reached the right number
    D. set a business-like tone at the beginning of the conversation

20. As soon as you pick up the phone, a very angry caller begins immediately to   20.____
complain about city agencies and *red tape*. He says that he has been shifted
to two or three different offices. It turs out that he is seeking information which
is not immediately available to you. You believe, you know, however, where it
can be found.
Which of the following actions is the BEST one for you to take?
    A. To eliminate all confusion, suggest that the caller write the agency stating
       explicitly what he wants.
    B. Apologize by telling the caller how busy city agencies now are, but also
       tell him directly that you do not have the information he needs.
    C. Ask for the caller's telephone number and assure him you will call back
       after you have checked further.
    D. Give the caller the name and telephone number of the person who might
       be able to help, but explain that you are not positive he will get results/

21. Which of the following approaches usually provides the BEST communication   21.____
in the objectives and values of a new program which is to be introduced?
    A. A general written description of the program by the program manager for
       review by those who share responsibility
    B. An effective verbal presentation by the program manager to those
       affected
    C. Development of the plan and operational approach in carrying out the
       program by the program manager assisted by his key subordinates
    D. Development of the plan by the program manager's supervisor

22. What is the BEST approach for introducing change?   22.____
A
    A. combination of written and also verbal communication to all personnel
       affected by the change
    B. general bulletin to all personnel
    C. meeting pointing out all the values of the new approach
    D. written directive to key personnel

23. Of the following, committees are BEST used for   23.____
    A. advising the head of the organization
    B. improving functional work
    C. making executive decisions
    D. making specific planning decisions

24. An effective discussion leader is one who 24.____
 A. announces the problem and his preconceived solution at the start of the discussion
 B. guides and directs the discussion according to pre-arranged outline
 C. interrupts or corrects confused participants to save time
 D. permits anyone to say anything at any time

25. The human relations movement in management theory is basically concerned 25.____
with
 A. counteracting employee unrest
 B. eliminating the *time and motion* man
 C. interrelationships among individuals in organizations
 D. the psychology of the worker

KEY (CORRECT ANSWERS)

1.	C		11.	A
2.	C		12.	B
3.	A		13.	B
4.	D		14.	D
5.	D		15.	D
6.	B		16.	C
7.	A		17.	D
8.	C		18.	B
9.	A		19.	C
10.	B		20.	C

21.	C
22.	A
23.	A
24.	B
25.	C

EXAMINATION SECTION
TEST 1

DIRECTIONS: Each question or incomplete statement is followed by several suggested answers or completions. Select the one that BEST answers the question or completes the statement. *PRINT THE LETTER OF THE CORRECT ANSWER IN THE SPACE AT THE RIGHT.*

1. In some agencies the counsel to the agency head is given the right to bypass the chain of command and issue orders directly to the staff concerning matters that involve certain specific processes and practices.
    This situation MOST nearly illustrates the principle of _____ authority.
    A. the acceptance theory of
    B. multiple-linear
    C. splintered
    D. functional

1._____

2. It is commonly understood that communication is an important part of the administrative process.
    Which of the following is NOT a valid principle of the communication process in administration?
    A. The channels of communication should be spontaneous.
    B. The lines of communication should be as direct and as short as possible.
    C. Communications should be authenticated.
    D. The persons serving in communications centers should be competent.

2._____

3. Of the following, the one factor which is generally considered LEAST essential to successful committee operations is
    A. stating a clear definition of the authority and scope of the committee
    B. selecting the committee chairman carefully
    C. limiting the size of the committee to four persons
    D. limiting the subject matter to that which can be handled in group discussion

3._____

4. Of the following, the failure by line managers to accept and appreciate the benefits and limitations of a new program or system VERY FREQUENTLY can be traced to the
    A. budgetary problems involved
    B. resultant need to reduce staff
    C. lack of controls it engenders
    D. failure of top management to support its implementation

4._____

5. If a manager were thinking about using a committee of subordinates to solve an operating problem, which of the following would generally NOT be an advantage of such use of the committee approach?
    A. Improved coordination
    B. Low cost
    C. Increased motivation
    D. Integrated judgment

5._____

6. Every supervisor has many occasions to lead a conference or participate in a conference of some sort.
Of the following statements that pertain to conferences and conference leadership, which is generally considered to be MOST valid?
   A. Since World War II, the trend has been toward fewer shared decisions and more conferences.
   B. The most important part of a conference leader's job is to direct discussion.
   C. In providing opportunities for group interaction, management should avoid consideration of its past management philosophy.
   D. A good administrator cannot lead a good conference if he is a poor public speaker.

6._____

7. Of the following, it is usually LEAST desirable for a conference leader to
   A. call the name of a person after asking a question
   B. summarize proceedings periodically
   C. make a practice of repeating questions
   D. ask a question without indicating who is to reply

7._____

8. Assume that, in a certain organization, a situation has developed in which there is little difference in status or authority between individuals.
Which of the following would be the MOST likely result with regard to communication in this organization?
   A. Both the accuracy and flow of communication will be improved.
   B. Both the accuracy and flow of communication will substantially decrease.
   C. Employees will seek more formal lines of communication.
   D. Neither the flow nor the accuracy of communication will be improved over the former hierarchical structure.

8._____

9. The main function of many agency administrative officers is "information management." Information that is received by an administrative officer may be classified as active or passive, depending upon whether or not it requires the recipient to take some action.
Of the following, the item received which is clearly the MOST active information is
   A. an appointment of a new staff member
   B. a payment voucher for a new desk
   C. a press release concerning a past event
   D. the minutes of a staff meeting

9._____

10. Of the following, the one LEAST considered to be a communication barrier is
   A. group feedback   B. charged words
   C. selective perception   D. symbolic meanings

10._____

11. Management studies support the hypothesis that, in spite of the tendency of employees to censor the information communicated to their supervisor, subordinates are more likely to communicate problem-oriented information UPWARD when they have a
    A. long period of service in the organization
    B. high degree of trust in the supervisor
    C. high educational level
    D. low status on the organizational ladder

11.____

12. Electronic data processing equipment can produce more information faster than can be generated by any other means.
    In view of this, the MOST important problem faced by management at present is to
    A. keep computers fully occupied
    B. find enough computer personnel
    C. assimilate and properly evaluate the information
    D. obtain funds to establish appropriate information systems

12.____

13. A well-designed management information system essentially provides each executive and manager the information he needs for
    A. determining computer time requirements
    B. planning and measuring results
    C. drawing a new organization chart
    D. developing a new office layout

13.____

14. It is generally agreed that management policies should be periodically reappraised and restated in accordance with current conditions.
    Of the following, the approach which would be MOST effective in determining whether a policy should be revised is to
    A. conduct interviews with staff members at all levels in order to ascertain the relationship between the policy and actual practice
    B. make proposed revisions in the policy and apply it to current problems
    C. make up hypothetical situations using both the old policy and a revised version in order to make comparisons
    D. call a meeting of top level staff in order to discuss ways of revising the policy

14.____

15. Your superior has asked you to notify division employees of an important change in one of the operating procedures described in the division manual. Every employee presently has a copy of this manual.
    Which of the following is normally the MOST practical way to get the employees to understand such a change?
    A. Notify each employee individually of the change and answer any questions he might have
    B. Send a written notice to key personnel, directing them to inform the people under them

15.____

C. Call a general meeting, distribute a corrected page for the manual, and discuss the change
D. Send a memo to employees describing the change in general terms and asking them to make the necessary corrections in their copies of the manual

16. Assume that the work in your department involves the use of any technical terms.
    In such a situation, when you are answering inquiries from the general public, it would usually be BEST to
    A. use simple language and avoid the technical terms
    B. employ the technical terms whenever possible
    C. bandy technical terms freely, but explain each term in parentheses
    D. apologize if you are forced to use a technical term

    16._____

17. Suppose that you receive a telephone call from someone identifying himself as an employee in another city department who asks to be given information which your own department regards as confidential.
    Which of the following is the BEST way of handling such a request?
    A. Give the information requested, since your caller as official standing
    B. Grant the request, provided the caller gives you a signed receipt
    C. Refuse the request, because you have no way of knowing whether the caller is really who he claims to be
    D. Explain that the information is confidential and inform the caller of the channels he must go through to have the information released to him

    17._____

18. Studies show that office employees place high importance on the social and human aspects of the organization. What office employees like best about their jobs is the kind of people with whom they work. So strive hard to group people who are most likely to get along well together.
    Based on this information, it is MOST reasonable to assume that office workers are most pleased to work in a group which
    A. is congenial   B. has high productivity
    C. allows individual creativity   D. is unlike other groups

    18._____

19. A certain supervisor does not compliment members of his staff when they come up with good ideas. He feels that coming up with good ideas is part of the job and does not merit special attention.
    This supervisor's practice is
    A. *poor*, because recognition for good ideas is a good motivator
    B. *poor*, because the staff will suspect that the supervisor has no good ideas of his own
    C. *good*, because it is reasonable to assume that employees will tell their supervisor of ways to improve office practice
    D. *good*, because the other members of the staff are not made to seem inferior by comparison

    19._____

20. Some employees of a department have sent an anonymous letter   20.____
containing many complaints to the department head.
Of the following, what is this MOST likely to show about the department?
    A. It is probably a good place to work.
    B. Communications are probably poor.
    C. The complaints are probably unjustified.
    D. These employees are probably untrustworthy.

21. Which of the following actions would usually be MOST appropriate for a   21.____
supervisor to take after receiving an instruction sheet from his superior
explaining a new procedure which is to be followed?
    A. Put the instruction sheet aside temporarily until he determines what is
        wrong with the old procedure.
    B. Call his superior and ask whether the procedure is one he must
        implement immediately.
    C. Write a memorandum to the superior asking for more details.
    D. Try the new procedure and advise the superior of any problems or
        possible improvements.

22. Of the following, which one is considered the PRIMARY advantage of   22.____
using a committee to resolved a problem in an organization?
    A. No one person will be held accountable for the decision since a group of
        people was involved.
    B. People with different backgrounds give attention to the problem.
    C. The decision will take considerable time so there is unlikely to be a
        decision that will later be regretted.
    D. One person cannot dominate the decision-making process.

23. Employees in a certain office come to their supervisor with all their   23.____
complaints about the office and the work. Almost every employee has had at
least one minor complaint at some time.
The situation with respect to complaints in this office may BEST be described
as probably
    A. *good*; employees who complain care about their jobs and work hard
    B. *good*; grievances brought out into the open can be corrected
    C. *bad*; only serious complaints should be discussed
    D. *bad*; it indicates the staff does not have confidence in the administration

24. The administrator who allows his staff to suggest ways to do their work   24.____
will usually find that
    A. this practice contributes to high productivity
    B. the administrator's ideas produce greater output
    C. clerical employees suggest inefficient work methods
    D. subordinate employees resent performing a management function

25. The MAIN purpose for a supervisor's questioning the employees at a conference he is holding is to
    A. stress those areas of information covered but not understood by the participants
    B. encourage participants to think through the problem under discussion
    C. catch those subordinates who are not paying attention
    D. permit the more knowledgeable participants to display their grasp of the problems being discussed

25.____

KEY (CORRECT ANSWERS)

1.	D		11.	B
2.	A		12.	C
3.	C		13.	B
4.	D		14.	A
5.	B		15.	C
6.	B		16.	A
7.	C		17.	D
8.	D		18.	A
9.	A		19.	A
10.	A		20.	B

21.	D
22.	B
23.	B
24.	A
25.	B

TEST 2

DIRECTIONS: Each question or incomplete statement is followed by several suggested answers or completions. Select the one that BEST answers the question or completes the statement. *PRINT THE LETTER OF THE CORRECT ANSWER IN THE SPACE AT THE RIGHT.*

1. For a superior to use *consultative supervision* with his subordinates effectively, it is ESSENTIAL that he   1.____
   A. accept the fact that his formal authority will be weakened by the procedure
   B. admit that he does not know more than all his men together and that his ideas are not always best
   C. utilize a committee system so that the procedure is orderly
   D. make sure that all subordinates are consulted so that no one feels left out

2. The *grapevine* is an informal means of communication in an organization. The attitude of a supervisor with respect to the grapevine should be to   2.____
   A. ignore it since it deals mainly with rumors and sensational information
   B. regard it as a serious danger which should be eliminated
   C. accept it as a real line of communication which should be listened to
   D. utilize it for most purposes instead of the official line of communication

3. The supervisor of an office that must deal with the public should realize that planning in this type of work situation   3.____
   A. is useless because he does not know how many people will request service or what service they will request
   B. must be done at a higher level but that he should be ready to implement the results of such planning
   C. is useful primarily for those activities that are not concerned with public contact
   D. is useful for all the activities of the office, including those that relate to public contact

4. Assume that it is your job to receive incoming telephone calls. Those calls which you cannot handle yourself have to be transferred to the appropriate office.   4.____
   If you receive an outside call for an extension line which is busy, the one of the following which you should do FIRST is to
   A. interrupt the person speaking on the extension and tell him a call is waiting
   B. tell the caller the line is busy and let him know every thirty seconds whether or not it is free
   C. leave the caller on "hold" until the extension is free
   D. tell the caller the line is busy and ask him if he wishes to wait

5. Your superior has subscribed to several publications directly related to your division's work, and he has asked you to see to it that the publications are circulated among the supervisory personnel in the division. There are eight supervisors involved.
The BEST method of insuring that all eight see these publications is to
   A. place the publication in the division's general reference library as soon as it arrives
   B. inform each supervisor whenever a publication arrives and remind all of them that they are responsible for reading it
   C. prepare a standard slip that can be stapled to each publication, listing the eight supervisors and saying, "Please read, initial your name, and pass along"
   D. send a memo to the eight supervisors saying that they may wish to purchase individual subscriptions in their own names if they are interested in seeing each issue

5.____

6. Your superior has telephoned a number of key officials in your agency to ask whether they can meet at a certain time next month. He has found that they can all make it, and he has asked you to confirm the meeting.
Which of the following is the BEST way to confirm such a meeting?
   A. Note the meeting on your superior's calendar.
   B. Post a notice of the meeting on the agency bulletin board.
   C. Call the officials on the day of the meeting to remind them of the meeting.
   D. Write a memo to each official involved, repeating the time and place of the meeting.

6.____

7. Assume that a new city regulation requires that certain kinds of private organizations file information forms with your department. You have been asked to write the short explanatory message that will be printed on the front cover of the pamphlet containing the forms and instructions.
Which of the following would be the MOST appropriate way of beginning this message?
   A. Get the readers' attention by emphasizing immediately that there are legal penalties for organizations that fail to file before a certain date.
   B. Briefly state the nature of the enclosed forms and the types of organizations that must file.
   C. Say that your department is very sorry to have to put organizations to such an inconvenience.
   D. Quote the entire regulation adopted by the city, even if it is quite long and is expressed din complicated legal language.

7.____

8. Suppose that you have been told to make up the vacation schedule for the 18 employees in a particular unit. In order for the unit to operate effectively, only a few employees can be on vacation at the same time.
Which of the following is the MOST advisable approach in making up the schedule?
   A. Draw up a schedule assigning vacations in alphabetical order
   B. Find out when the supervisors want to take their vacations, and randomly assign whatever periods are left to the non-supervisory personnel

8.____

    C. Assign the most desirable times to employees of longest standing and the least desirable times to the newest employees

    D. Have all employees state their own preference, and then work out any conflicts in consultation with the people involved

9. Assume that you have been asked to prepare job descriptions for various positions in your department.
Which of the following are the basic points that should be covered in a *job description*?
    A. General duties and responsibilities of the position, with examples of day-to-day tasks
    B. Comments on the performances of present employees
    C. Estimates of the number of openings that may be available in each category during the coming year
    D. Instructions for carrying out the specific tasks assigned to your department

    9._____

10. Of the following, the biggest DISADVANTAGE in allowing a free flow of communications in an agency is that such a free flow
    A. decreases creativity
    B. increases the use of the *grapevine*
    C. lengthens the chain of command
    D. reduces the executive's power to direct the flow of information

    10._____

11. A downward flow of authority in an organization is one example of _____ communication.
    A. horizontal   B. informal   C. circular   D. vertical

    11._____

12. Of the following, the one that would MOST likely block effective communication is
    A. concentration only on the issues at hand
    B. lack of interest or commitment
    C. use of written reports
    D. use of charts and graphs

    12._____

13. An ADVANTAGE of the *lecture* as a teaching tool is that it
    A. enables a person to present his ideas to a large number of people
    B. allows the audience to retain a maximum of the information given
    C. holds the attention of the audience for the longest time
    D. enables the audience member to easily recall the main points

    13._____

14. An ADVANTAGE of the *small-group* discussion as a teaching tool is that
    A. it always focuses attention on one person as the leader
    B. it places collective responsibility on the group as a whole
    C. its members gain experience by summarizing the ideas of others
    D. each member of the group acts as a member of a team

    14._____

15. The one of the following that is an ADVANTAGE of a *large-group* discussion,   15._____
when compared to a small-group discussion, is that the large-group discussion
  A. moves along more quickly than a small-group discussion
  B. allows its participants to feel more at ease, and speak out more freely
  C. gives the whole group a chance to exchange ideas on a certain subject at the same occasion
  D. allows its members to feel a greater sense of personal responsibility

———————

KEY (CORRECT ANSWERS)

1.	D	6.	D	11.	D
2.	C	7.	B	12.	B
3.	D	8.	D	13.	A
4.	D	9.	A	14.	D
5.	C	10.	D	15.	C

———————

CLERICAL ABILITIES

EXAMINATION SECTION

TEST 1

DIRECTIONS: Each question or incomplete statement is followed by several suggested answers or completions. Select the one that BEST answers the question or completes the statement. *PRINT THE LETTER OF THE CORRECT ANSWER IN THE SPACE AT THE RIGHT.*

Questions 1-4.

DIRECTIONS: Questions 1 through 4 are to be answered on the basis of the information given below.

The most commonly used filing system and the one that is easiest to learn is alphabetical filing. This involves putting records in an A to Z order, according to the letters of the alphabet. The name of a person is filed by using the following order: first, the surname or last name; second, the first name; third, the middle name or middle initial. For example, *Henry C. Young* is filed under *Y* and thereafter under *Young, Henry C.* The name of a company is filed in the same way. For example, *Long Cabinet Co.* is filed under *L* while *John T. Long Cabinet Co.* is filed under *L* and thereafter under *Long, John T. Cabinet Co.*

1. The one of the following which lists the names of persons in the CORRECT   1.____
   alphabetical order is:
   A. Mary Carrie, Helen Carrol, James Carson, John Carter
   B. James Carson, Mary Carrie, John Carter, Helen Carrol
   C. Helen Carrol, James Carson, John Carter, Mary Carrie
   D. John Carter, Helen Carrol, Mary Carrie, James Carson

2. The one of the following which lists the names of persons in the CORRECT   2.____
   alphabetical order is:
   A. Jones, John C.; Jones, John A.; Jones, John P.; Jones, John K.
   B. Jones, John P.; Jones, John K.; Jones, John C.; Jones, John A.
   C. Jones, John A.; Jones, John C.; Jones, John K.; Jones, John P.
   D. Jones, John K.; Jones, John C.; Jones, John A.; Jones, John P.

3. The one of the following which lists the names of the companies in the   3.____
   CORRECT alphabetical order is:
   A. Blane Co., Blake Co., Block Co., Blear Co.
   B. Blake Co., Blane Co., Blear Co., Block Co.
   C. Block Co., Blear Co., Blane Co., Blake Co.
   D. Blear Co., Blake Co., Blane Co., Block Co.

4. You are to return to the file an index card on *Barry C. Wayne Materials and Supplies Co.*
   Of the following, the CORRECT alphabetical group that you should return the index card to is
      A. A to G   B. H to M   C. N to S   D. T to Z

4.____

Questions 5-10.

DIRECTIONS: In each of Questions 5 through 10, the names of four people are given. For each question, choose as your answer the one of the four names given which should be filed FIRST according to the usual system of alphabetical filing of names, as described in the following paragraph.

    In filing names, you must start with the last name. Names are filed in order of the first letter of the last name, then the second letter, etc. Therefore, BAILY would be filed before BROWN, which would be filed before COLT. A name with fewer letters of the same type comes first, i.e., Smith before Smithe. If the last names are the same, the names are filed alphabetically by the first name. If the first name is an initial, a name with an initial would come before a first name that starts with the same letter as the initial. Therefore, I. BROWN would come before IRA BROWN. Finally, if both last name and first name are the same, the name would be filed alphabetically by the middle name, once again an initial coming before a middle name which starts with the same letter as the initial. If there is no middle name at all, the name would come before those with middle initials or names.

        SAMPLE QUESTION: A. Lester Daniels
                                   B. William Dancer
                                   C. Nathan Danzig
                                   D. Dan Lester

    The last names beginning with D are filed before the last name beginning with L. Since DANIELS, DANCER, and DANZIG all begin with the same three letters, you must look at the fourth letter of the last name to determine which name should be filed first. C comes before I or Z in the alphabet, so DANCER is filed before DANIELS or DANZIG. Therefore, the answer to the above sample question is B.

5.   A.   Scott Biala
       B.   Mary Byala
       C.   Martin Baylor
       D.   Francis Bauer

5.____

6.   A.   Howard J. Black
       B.   Howard Black
       C.   J. Howard Black
       D.   John H. Black

6.____

7.   A.   Theodora Garth Kingston
       B.   Theadore Barth Kingston
       C.   Thomas Kingston
       D.   Thomas T. Kingston

7.____

8. A.   Paulette Mary Huerta
    B.   Paul M. Huerta
    C.   Paulette L. Huerta
    D.   Peter A. Huerta

8._____

9. A.   Martha Hunt Morgan
    B.   Martin Hunt Morgan
    C.   Mary H. Morgan
    D.   Martine H. Morgan

9._____

10. A.   James T. Meerschaum
    B.   James M. Mershum
    C.   James F. Mearshaum
    D.   James N. Meshum

10._____

Questions 11-14.

DIRECTIONS: Questions 11 through 14 are to be answered SOLELY on the basis of the
                      following information.

     You are required to file various documents in file drawers which are labeled according to
the following pattern:

DOCUMENTS

MEMOS		LETTERS	
File	Subject	File	Subject
84PM1	(A-L)	84PC1	(A-L)
84PM2	(M-Z)	84PC2	(M-Z)

REPORTS		INQUIRIES	
File	Subject	File	Subject
84PR1	(A-L)	84PQ1	(A-L)
84PR2	(M-Z)	84PQ2	(M-Z)

11. A letter dealing with a burglary should be filed in the drawer labeled
    A. 84PM1   B. 84PC1   C. 84PR1   D. 84PQ2

11._____

12. A report on Statistics should be found in the drawer labeled
    A. 84PM1   B. 84PC2   C. 84PR2   D. 84PQS

12._____

13. An inquiry is received about parade permit procedures. It should be filed in
    the drawer labeled
    A. 84PM2   B. 84PC1   C. 84PR1   D. 84PQ2

13._____

14. A police officer has a question about a robbery report you filed.
    You should pull this file from the drawer labeled
    A. 84PM1   B. 84PM2   C. 84PR1   D. 84PR2

14._____

Questions 15-22.

DIRECTIONS: Each of Questions 15 through 22 consists of four or six numbered names. For each question, choose the option (A, B, C, or D) which indicates the order in which the names should be filed in accordance with the following filing instructions:
- File alphabetically according to last name, then first name, then middle initial.
- File according to each successive letter within a name.
- When comparing two names in which the letters in the longer name are identical to the corresponding letters in the shorter name, the shorter name is filed first.
- When the last names are the same, initials are always filed before names beginning with the same letter.

15. I.   Ralph Robinson
    II. Alfred Ross
    III. Luis Robles
    IV. James Roberts

    The CORRECT filing sequence for the above names should be
    A. IV, II, I, III   B. I, IV, III, II   C. III, IV, I, II   D. IV, I, III, II

16. I.   Irwin Goodwin
    II. Inez Gonzalez
    III. Irene Goodman
    IV. Ira S. Goodwin
    V.   Ruth I. Goldstein
    VI. M.B. Goodman

    The CORRECT filing sequence for the above names should be
    A. V, II, I, IV, III, VI   B. V, II, VI, III, IV, I
    C. V, II, III, VI, IV, I   D. V, II, III, VI, I, IV

17. I.   George Allan
    II. Gregory Allen
    III. Gary Allen
    IV. George Allen

    The CORRECT filing sequence for the above names should be
    A. IV, III, I, II   B. I, IV, II, III   C. III, IV, I, II   D. I, III, IV, II

18. I.   Simon Kauffman   18.____
     II.   Leo Kaufman
     III. Robert Kaufmann
     IV.   Paul Kauffmann

     The CORRECT filing sequence for the above names should be
       A. I, IV, II, III   B. II, IV, III, I   C. III, II, IV, I   D. I, II, III, IV

19. I.   Roberta Williams   19.____
     II.   Robin Wilson
     III. Roberta Wilson
     IV.   Robin Williams

     The CORRECT filing sequence for the above names should be
       A. III, II, IV, I   B. I, IV, III, II   C. I, II, III, IV   D. III, I, II, IV

20. I.   Lawrence Shultz   20.____
     II.   Albert Schultz
     III. Theodore Schwartz
     IV.   Thomas Schwarz
     V.   Alvin Schultz
     VI.   Leonard Shultz

     The CORRECT filing sequence for the above names should be
       A. II, V, III, IV, I, VI   B. IV, III, V, I, II, VI
       C. II, V, I, VI, III, IV   D. I, VI, II, V, III, IV

21. I.   McArdle   21.____
     II.   Mayer
     III. Maletz
     IV.   McNiff
     V.   Meyer
     VI.   MacMahon

     The CORRECT filing sequence for the above names should be
       A. I, IV, VI, III, II, V   B. II, I, IV, VI, III, V
       C. VI, III, II, I, IV, V   D. VI, III, II, V, I, IV

22. I.   Jack E. Johnson   22.____
     II.   R.H. Jackson
     III. Bertha Jackson
     IV.   J.T. Johnson
     V.   Ann Johns
     VI.   John Jacobs

     The CORRECT filing sequence for the above names should be
       A. II, III, VI, V, IV, I   B. III, II, VI, V, IV, I
       C. VI, II, III, I, V, IV   D. III, II, VI, IV, V, I

Questions 23-30.

DIRECTIONS: The code table below shows 10 letters with matching numbers. For each question, there are three sets of letters. Each set of letters is followed by a set of numbers which may or may not match their correct letter according to the code table. For each question, check all three sets of letters and numbers and mark your answer:
A. if no pairs are correctly matched
B. if only one pair is correctly matched
C. if only two pairs are correctly matched
D. if all three pairs are correctly matched

CODE TABLE

T	M	V	D	S	P	R	G	B	H
1	2	3	4	5	6	7	8	9	0

SAMPLE QUESTION:
TMVDSP – 123456
RGBHTM – 789011
DSPRGB – 256789

In the sample question above, the first set of numbers correctly match its set of letters. But the second and third pairs contain mistakes. In the second pair, M is correctly matched with number 1. According to the code table, letter M should be correctly matched with number 2. In the third pair, the letter D is incorrectly matched with number 2. According to the code table, letter D should be correctly matched with number 4. Since only one of the pairs is correctly matched, the answer to this sample question is B.

23. RSBMRM – 759262
    GDSRVH – 845730
    VDBRTM - 349713

23.____

24. TGVSDR – 183247
    SMHRDP – 520647
    TRMHSR - 172057

24.____

25. DSPRGM – 456782
    MVDBHT – 234902
    HPMDBT - 062491

25.____

26. BVPTRD – 936184
    GDPHMB – 807029
    GMRHMV - 827032

26.____

27. MGVRSH – 283750
    TRDMBS – 174295
    SPRMGV - 567283

27.____

28. SGBSDM – 489542
MGHPTM – 290612
MPBMHT - 269301

28.____

29. TDPBHM – 146902
VPBMRS – 369275
GDMBHM - 842902

29.____

30. MVPTBV – 236194
PDRTMB – 47128
BGTMSM - 981232

30.____

KEY (CORRECT ANSWERS)

1.	A	11.	B	21.	C
2.	C	12.	C	22.	B
3.	B	13.	D	23.	B
4.	D	14.	D	24.	B
5.	D	15.	D	25.	C
6.	B	16.	C	26.	A
7.	B	17.	D	27.	D
8.	B	18.	A	28.	A
9.	A	19.	B	29.	D
10.	C	20.	A	30.	A

TEST 2

DIRECTIONS: Each question or incomplete statement is followed by several suggested answers or completions. Select the one that BEST answers the question or completes the statement. *PRINT THE LETTER OF THE CORRECT ANSWER IN THE SPACE AT THE RIGHT.*

Questions 1-10.

DIRECTIONS: Questions 1 through 10 each consists of two columns, each containing four lines of names, numbers and/or addresses. For each question, compare the lines in Column I with the lines in Column II to see if they match exactly, and mark your answer A, B, C, or D, according to the following instructions:
- A. all four lines match exactly
- B. only three lines match exactly
- C. only two lines match exactly
- D. only one line matches exactly

	COLUMN I	COLUMN II	
1.	I. Earl Hodgson II. 1409870 III. Shore Ave. IV. Macon Rd.	Earl Hodgson 1408970 Schore Ave. Macon Rd.	1.____
2.	I. 9671485 II. 470 Astor Court III. Halprin, Phillip IV. Frank D. Poliseo	9671485 470 Astor Court Halperin, Phillip Frank D. Poliseo	2.____
3.	I. Tandem Associates II. 144-17 Northern Blvd. III. Alberta Forchi IV. Kings Park, NY 10751	Tandom Associates 144-17 Northern Blvd. Albert Forchi Kings Point, NY 10751	3.____
4.	I. Bertha C. McCormack II. Clayton, MO III. 976-4242 IV. New City, NY 10951	Bertha C. McCormack Clayton, MO 976-4242 New City, NY 10951	4.____
5.	I. George C. Morill II. Columbia, SC 29201 III. Louis Ingham IV. 3406 Forest Ave.	George C. Morrill Columbia, SD 29201 Louis Ingham 3406 Forest Ave.	5.____
6.	I. 506 S. Elliott Pl. II. Herbert Hall III. 4712 Rockaway Pkway IV. 169 E. 7 St.	506 S. Elliott Pl. Hurbert Hall 4712 Rockaway Pkway 169 E. 7 St.	6.____

7.	I.	345 Park Ave.	345 Park Pl.	7.____
	II.	Colman Oven Corp.	Coleman Oven Corp.	
	III.	Robert Conte	Robert Conti	
	IV.	6179846	6179846	

8.	I.	Grigori Schierber	Grigori Schierber	8.____
	II.	Des Moines, Iowa	Des Moines, Iowa	
	III.	Gouverneur Hospital	Gouverneur Hospital	
	IV.	91-35 Cresskill Pl.	91-35 Cresskill Pl.	

9.	I.	Jeffery Janssen	Jeffrey Janssen	9.____
	II.	8041071	8041071	
	III.	40 Rockefeller Plaza	40 Rockafeller Plaza	
	IV.	407 6 St.	406 7 St.	

10.	I.	5971996	5871996	10.____
	II.	3113 Knickerbocker Ave.	31123 Knickerbocker Ave.	
	III.	8434 Boston Post Rd.	8424 Boston Post Rd.	
	IV.	Penn Station	Penn Station	

Questions 11-14.

DIRECTIONS: Questions 11 through 14 are to be answered by looking at the four groups of names and addresses listed below (I, II, III, and IV), and then finding out the number of groups that have their corresponding numbered lies exactly the same.

	GROUP I	GROUP II
Line 1.	Richmond General Hospital	Richman General Hospital
Line 2.	Geriatric Clinic	Geriatric Clinic
Line 3.	3975 Paerdegat St.	3975 Peardegat St.
Line 4.	Loudonville, New York 11538	Londonville, New York 11538

	GROUP III	GROUP IV
Line 1.	Richmond General Hospital	Rikchmend General Hospital
Line 2.	Geriatric Clinic	Geriatric Clinic
Line 3.	3795 Paerdegat St.	3975 Paerdegat St.
Line 4.	Loudonville, New York 11358	Loudonville, New York 11538

1. In how many groups is line one exactly the same?   11.____
     A. Two   B. Three   C. Four   D. None

12. In how many groups is line two exactly the same?   12.____
     A. Two   B. Three   C. Four   D. None

13. In how many groups is line three exactly the same?   13.____
     A. Two   B. Three   C. Four   D. None

14. In how many groups is line four exactly the same?   14._____
    A. Two   B. Three   C. Four   D. None

Questions 15-18.

DIRECTIONS: Each of Questions 15 through 18 has two lists of names and addresses. Each
              list contains three sets of names and addresses. Check each of the three sets
              in the list on the right to see if they are the same as the corresponding set in
              the list on the left. Mark your answers:
                  A. if none of the sets in the right list are the same as those in the left list
                  B. if only one of the sets in the right list is the same as those in the left list
                  C. if only two of the sets in the right list are the same as those in the left list
                  D. if all three sets in the right list are the same as those in the left list

15.   Mary T. Berlinger   Mary T. Berlinger   15._____
      2351 Hampton St.   2351 Hampton St.
      Monsey, N.Y. 20117   Monsey, N.Y. 20117

      Eduardo Benes   Eduardo Benes
      483 Kingston Avenue   473 Kingston Avenue
      Central Islip, N.Y. 11734   Central Islip, N.Y. 11734

      Alan Carrington Fuchs   Alan Carrington Fuchs
      17 Gnarled Hollow Road   17 Gnarled Hollow Road
      Los Angeles, CA 91635   Los Angeles, CA 91685

16.   David John Jacobson   David John Jacobson   16._____
      178 34 St. Apt. 4C   178 53 St. Apt. 4C
      New York, N.Y. 00927   New York, N.Y. 00927

      Ann-Marie Calonella   Ann-Marie Calonella
      7243 South Ridge Blvd.   7243 South Ridge Blvd.
      Bakersfield, CA 96714   Bakersfield, CA 96714

      Pauline M. Thompson   Pauline M. Thomson
      872 Linden Ave.   872 Linden Ave.
      Houston, Texas 70321   Houston, Texas 70321

17.   Chester LeRoy Masterton   Chester LeRoy Masterson   17._____
      152 Lacy Rd.   152 Lacy Rd.
      Kankakee, Ill. 54532   Kankakee, Ill. 54532

      William Maloney   William Maloney
      S. LaCrosse Pla.   S. LaCross Pla.
      Wausau, Wisconsin 52136   Wausau, Wisconsin 52146

      Cynthia V. Barnes   Cynthia V. Barnes
      16 Pines Rd.   16 Pines Rd.
      Greenpoint, Miss. 20376   Greenpoint,, Miss. 20376

18. Marcel Jean Frontenac   Marcel Jean Frontenac   18._____
     8 Burton On The Water   6 Burton On The Water
     Calender, Me. 01471   Calender, Me. 01471

     J. Scott Marsden   J. Scott Marsden
     174 S. Tipton St.   174 Tipton St.
     Cleveland, Ohio   Cleveland, Ohio

     Lawrence T. Haney   Lawrence T. Haney
     171 McDonough St.   171 McDonough St.
     Decatur, Ga. 31304   Decatur, Ga. 31304

Questions 19-26.

DIRECTIONS: Each of Questions 19 through 26 has two lists of numbers. Each list contains three sets of numbers. Check each of the three sets in the list on the right to see if they are the same as the corresponding set in the list on the left. Mark your answers:

     A. if none of the sets in the right list are the same as those in the left list
     B. if only one of the sets in the right list is the same as those in the left list
     C. if only two of the sets in the right list are the same as those in the left list
     D. if all three sets in the right list are the same as those in the left lists

19. 7354183476   7354983476   19._____
     4474747744   4474747774
     5791430231   57914302311

20. 7143592185   7143892185   20._____
     8344517699   8344518699
     9178531263   9178531263

21. 2572114731   257214731   21._____
     8806835476   8806835476
     8255831246   8255831246

22. 331476853821   331476858621   22._____
     6976658532996   6976655832996
     3766042113715   3766042113745

23. 8806663315   88066633115   23._____
     74477138449   74477138449
     211756663666   211756663666

24. 990006966996   99000696996   24.____
    53022219743   53022219843
    4171171117717   4171171177717

25. 24400222433004   24400222433004   25.____
    5300030055000355   5300030055500355
    20000075532002022   20000075532002022

26. 611166640660001116   61116664066001116   26.____
    7111300117001100733   7111300117001100733
    26666446664476518   26666446664476518

Questions 27-30.

DIRECTIONS: Questions 27 through 30 are to be answered by picking the answer which is in the correct numerical order, from the lowest number to the highest number, in each question.

27. A. 44533, 44518, 44516, 44547   27.____
    B. 44516, 44518, 44533, 44547
    C. 44547, 44533, 44518, 44516
    D. 44518, 44516, 44547, 44533

28. A. 95587, 95593, 95601, 95620   28.____
       95601, 95620, 95587, 95593
       95593, 95587, 95601. 95620
       95620, 95601, 95593, 95587

29.   232212, 232208, 232232, 232223   29.____
       232208, 232223, 232212, 232232
       232208, 232212, 232223, 232232
       232223, 232232, 232208, 232208

30.   113419, 113521, 113462, 113462   30.____
       113588, 113462, 113521, 113419
       113521, 113588, 113419, 113462
       113419, 113462, 113521, 113588

KEY (CORRECT ANSWERS)

1.	C	11.	A	21.	C
2.	B	12.	C	22.	A
3.	D	13.	A	23.	D
4.	A	14.	A	24.	A
5.	C	15.	C	25.	C
6.	B	16.	B	26.	C
7.	D	17.	B	27.	B
8.	A	18.	B	28.	A
9.	D	19.	B	29.	C
10.	C	20.	B	30.	D

RECORD KEEPING
EXAMINATION SECTION
TEST 1

DIRECTIONS: Each question or incomplete statement is followed by several suggested answers or completions. Select the one that BEST answers the question or completes the statement. *PRINT THE LETTER OF THE CORRECT ANSWER IN THE SPACE AT THE RIGHT.*

Questions 1-7.

DIRECTIONS: In answering Questions 1 through 7, use the following master list. For each question, determine where the name would fit on the master list. Each answer choice indicates right before or after the name in the answer choice.

        Aaron, Jane
        Armstead, Brendan
        Bailey, Charles
        Dent, Ricardo
        Grant, Mark
        Mars, Justin
        Methieu, Justine
        Parker, Cathy
        Sampson, Suzy
        Thomas, Heather

1.   Schmidt, William   1.____
      A. Right before Cathy Parker   B. Right after Heather Thomas
      C. Right after Suzy Sampson   D. Right before Ricardo Dent

2.   Asanti, Kendall   2.____
      A. Right before Jane Aaron   B. Right after Charles Bailey
      C. Right before Justine Methieu   D. Right after Brendan Armstead

3.   O'Brien, Daniel   3.____
      A. Right after Justine Methieu   B. Right before Jane Aaron
      C. Right after Mark Grant   D. Right before Suzy Sampson

4.   Marrow, Alison   4.____
      A. Right before Cathy Parker   B. Right before Justin Mars
      C. Right after Mark Grant   D. Right after Heather Thomas

5.   Grantt, Marissa   5.____
      A. Right before Mark Grant   B. Right after Mark Grant
      C. Right after Justin Mars   D. Right before Suzy Sampson

6. Thompson, Heath   6.____
    A. Right after Justin Mars   B. Right before Suzy Sampson
    C. Right after Heather Thomas   D. Right before Cathy Parker

DIRECTIONS: Before answering Question 7, add in all of the names from Questions 1 through
              6. Then fit the name in alphabetical order based on the new list.

7. Francisco, Mildred   7.____
    A. Right before Mark Grant   B. Right after Marissa Grantt
    C. Right before Alison Marrow   D. Right after Kendall Asanti

Questions 8-10.

DIRECTIONS: In answering Questions 8 through 10, compare each pair of names and
              addresses. Indicate whether they are the same or different in any way.

8. William H. Pratt, J.D.   William H. Pratt, J.D.   8.____
    Attourney at Law   Attorney at Law
    A. No differences   B. 1 difference
    C. 2 differences   D. 3 differences

9. 1303 Theater Drive,; Apt. 3-B   1330 Theatre Drive,; Apt. 3-B   9.____
    A. No differences   B. 1 difference
    C. 2 differences   D. 3 differences

10. Petersdorff, Briana and Mary   Petersdorff, Briana and Mary   10.____
    A. No differences   B. 1 difference
    C. 2 differences   D. 3 differences

11. Which of the following words, if any, are misspelled?   11.____
    A. Affordable   B. Circumstansial
    C. Legalese   D. None of the above

Questions 12-13.

DIRECTIONS: Questions 12 and 13 are to be answered on the basis of the following table.

Standardized Test Results for High School Students in District #1230

	English	Math	Science	Reading
High School 1	21	22	15	18
High School 2	12	16	13	15
High School 3	16	18	21	17
High School 4	19	14	15	16

The scores for each high school in the district were averaged out and listed for each
subject tested. Scores of 0-10 are significantly below College Readiness Standards. 11-15 are
below College Readiness, 16-20 meet College Readiness, and 21-25 are above College
Readiness.

12. If the high schools need to meet or exceed in at least half the categories
in order to NOT be considered "at risk," which schools are considered "at risk"?
 A. High School 2   B. High School 3
 C. High School 4   D. Both A and C

12.____

13. What percentage of subjects did the district as a whole meet or exceed
College Readiness standards?
 A. 25% B. 50% C. 75% D. 100%

13.____

Questions 14-15.

DIRECTIONS: Questions 14 and 15 are to be answered on the basis of the following
information.

You have seven employees working as a part of your team: Austin, Emily, Jeremy,
Christina, Martin, Harriet, and Steve. You have just sent an e-mail informing them that
there will be a mandatory training session next week. To ensure that work still gets done,
you are offering the training twice during the week: once on Tuesday and also on
Thursday. This way half the employees will still be working while the other half attend the
training. The only other issue is that Jeremy doesn't work on Tuesdays and Harriet
doesn't work on Thursdays due to compressed work schedules.

14. Which of the following is a possible attendance roster for the first training
session?
 A. Emily, Jeremy, Steve   B. Steve, Christina, Harriet
 C. Harriet, Jeremy, Austin   D. Steve, Martin, Jeremy

14.____

15. If Harriet, Christina, and Steve attend the training session on Tuesday, which
of the following is a possible roster for Thursday's training session?
 A. Jeremy, Emily, and Austin   B. Emily, Martin, and Harriet
 C. Austin, Christina, and Emily   D. Jeremy, Emily, and Steve

15.____

Questions 16-20.

DIRECTIONS: In answering Questions 16 through 20, you will be given a word and will need
to choose the answer choice that is MOST similar or different to the word.

16. Which word means the SAME as *annual*?
 A. Monthly B. Usually C. Yearly D. Constantly

16.____

17. Which word means the SAME as *effort*?
 A. Energy B. Equate C. Cherish D. Commence

17.____

18. Which word means the OPPOSITE of *forlorn*?
 A. Neglected B. Lethargy C. Optimistic D. Astonished

18.____

19. Which word means the SAME as *risk*?
 A. Admire B. Hazard C. Limit D. Hesitant

19.____

20. Which word means the OPPOSITE of *translucent*?   20.____
    A. Opaque   B. Transparent   C. Luminous   D. Introverted

21. Last year, Jamie's annual salary was $50,000. Her boss called her today   21.____
    to inform her that she would receive a 20% raise for the upcoming year. How
    much more money will Jamie receive next year?
    A. $60,000   B. $10,000   C. $1,000   D. $51,000

22. You and a co-worker work for a temp hiring agency as part of their office   22.____
    staff. You both are given 6 days off per month. How many days off are you
    and your co-worker given in a year?
    A. 24   B. 72   C. 144   D. 48

23. If Margot makes $34,000 per year and she works 40 hours per week for   23.____
    all 52 weeks, what is her hourly rate?
    A. $16.34/hour   B. $17.00/hour   C. $15.54/hour   D. $13.23/hour

24. How many dimes are there in $175.00?   24.____
    A. 175   B. 1,750   C. 3,500   D. 17,500

25. If Janey is three times as old as Emily, and Emily is 3, how old is Janey?   25.____
    A. 6   B. 9   C. 12   D. 15

KEY (CORRECT ANSWERS)

1.	C		11.	B
2.	D		12.	A
3.	A		13.	D
4.	B		14.	B
5.	B		15.	A
6.	C		16.	C
7.	A		17.	A
8.	B		18.	C
9.	C		19.	B
10.	A		20.	A

21.	B
22.	C
23.	A
24.	B
25.	B

TEST 2

DIRECTIONS: Each question or incomplete statement is followed by several suggested answers or completions. Select the one that BEST answers the question or completes the statement. *PRINT THE LETTER OF THE CORRECT ANSWER IN THE SPACE AT THE RIGHT.*

Questions 1-6.

DIRECTIONS: Questions 1 through 6 are to be answered on the basis of the following information.

item	name of item to be ordered
quantity	minimum number that can be ordered
beginning amount	amount in stock at start of month
amount received	amount receiving during month
ending amount	amount in stock at end of month
amount used	amount used during month
amount to order	will need at least as much of each item as used in the previous month
unit price	cost of each unit of an item
total price	total price for the order

Item	Quantity	Beginning	Received	Ending	Amount Used	Amount to Order	Unit Price	Total Price
Pens	10	22	10	8	24	20	$0.11	$2.20
Spiral notebooks	8	30	13	12			$0.25	
Binder clips	2 boxes	3 boxes	1 box	1 box			$1.79	
Sticky notes	3 packs	12 packs	4 packs	2 packs			$1.29	
Dry erase markers	1 pack (dozen)	34 markers	8 markers	40 markers			$16.49	
Ink cartridges (printer)	1 cartridge	3 cartridges	1 cartridge	2 cartridges			$79.99	
Folders	10 folders	25 folders	15 folders	10 folders			$1.08	

1. How many packs of sticky notes were used during the month?   1.____
   A. 16   B. 10   C. 12   D. 14

2. How many folders need to be ordered for next month?   2.____
   A. 15   B. 20   C. 30   D. 40

3. What is the total price of notebooks that you will need to order?   3.____
   A. $6.00   B. $0.25   C. $4.50   D. $2.75

4. Which of the following will you spend the second most money on?   4.____
   A. Ink cartridges   B. Dry erase markers
   C. Sticky notes   D. Binder clips

5. How many packs of dry erase markers should you order?   5.____
   A. 1   B. 8   C. 12   D. 0

6. What will be the total price of the file folders you order? 6._____
    A. $20.16   B. $21.60   C. $10.00   D. $4.32

Questions 7-11.

DIRECTIONS: Questions 7 through 11 are to be answered on the basis of the following table.

Number of Car Accidents, By Location and Cause, for 2014						
	Location 1		Location 2		Location 3	
Cause	Number	Percent	Number	Percent	Number	Percent
Severe Weather	10		25		30	
Excessive Speeding	20	40	5		10	
Impaired Driving	15		15	25	8	
Miscellaneous	5		15		2	4
TOTALS	50	100	60	100	50	100

7. Which of the following is the third highest cause of accidents for all three 7._____
    locations?
    A. Severe Weather   B. Impaired Driving
    C. Miscellaneous   D. Excessive Speeding

8. The average number of Severe Weather accidents per week at Location 3 8._____
    for the year (52 weeks) was MOST NEARLY
    A. 0.57   B. 30   C. 1   D. 1.25

9. Which location had the LARGEST percentage of accidents caused by 9._____
    Impaired Driving?
    A. 1   B. 2   C. 3   D. Both A and B

10. If one-third of the accidents at all three locations resulted in at least one 10._____
    fatality, what is the LEAST amount of deaths caused by accidents last year?
    A. 60   B. 106   C. 66   D. 53

11. What is the percentage of accidents caused by miscellaneous means from 11._____
    all three locations in 2014?
    A. 5%   B. 10%   C. 13%   D. 25%

12. How many pairs of the following groups of letters are exactly alike? 12._____
    ACDOBJ   ACDBOJ
    HEWBWR   HEWRWB
    DEERVS   DEERVS
    BRFQSX   BRFQSX
    WEYRVB   WEYRVB
    SPQRZA   SQRPZA

    A. 2   B. 3   C. 4   D. 5

Questions 13-19.

DIRECTIONS: Questions 13 through 19 are to be answered on the basis of the following
              information.

       In 2012, the most current information on the American population was finished. The
information was compiled by 200 volunteers in each of the 50 states. The territory of Puerto
Rico, a sovereign of the United States, had 25 people assigned to compile data. In February of
2010, volunteers in each state and sovereign began collecting information. In Puerto Rico, data
collection finished by January 31st, 2011, while work in the United States was completed on
June 30, 2012. Each volunteer gathered data on the population of their state or sovereign.
When the information was compiled, volunteers sent reports to the nation's capital, Washington,
D.C. Each volunteer worked 20 hours per month and put together 10 reports per month. After
the data was compiled in total, 50 people reviewed the data and worked from January 2012 to
December 2012.

13.   How many reports were generated from February 2010 to April 2010 in Illinois   13.____
      and Ohio?
         A. 3,000   B. 6,000   C. 12,000   D. 15,000

14.   How many volunteers in total collected population data in January 2012?   14.____
         A. 10,000   B. 2,000   C. 225   D. 200

15.   How many reports were put together in May 2012?   15.____
         A. 2,000   B. 50,000   C. 100,000   D. 100,250

16.   How many hours did the Puerto Rican volunteers work in the fall   16.____
      (September-November)?
         A. 60   B. 500   C. 1,500   D. 0

17.   How many workers were compiling or reviewing data in July 2012?   17.____
         A. 25   B. 50   C. 200   D. 250

18.   What was the total amount of hours worked by Nevada volunteers in July 2010?   18.____
         A. 500   B. 4,000   C. 4,500   D. 5,000

19.   How many reviewers worked in January 2013?   19.____
         A. 75   B. 50   C. 0   D. 25

20.   John has to file 10 documents per shelf. How many documents would it   20.____
      take for John to fill 40 shelves?
         A. 40   B. 400   C. 4,500   D. 5,000

21.   Jill wants to travel from New York City to Los Angeles by bike, which   21.____
      is approximately 2,772 miles. How many miles per day would Jill need to
      average if she wanted to complete the trip in 4 weeks?
         A. 100   B. 89   C. 99   D. 94

22. If there are 24 CPU's and only 7 monitors, how many more monitors do you need to have the same amount of monitors as CPU's?
   A. Not enough information   B. 17
   C. 31   D. 0
22._____

23. If Gerry works 5 days a week and 8 hours each day, and John works 3 days a week and 10 hours each day, how many more hours per year will Gerry work than John?
   A. They work the same amount of hours.
   B. 450
   C. 520
   D. 832
23._____

24. Jimmy gets transferred to a new office. The new office has 25 employees, but only 16 are there due to a blizzard. How many coworkers was Jimmy able to meet on his first day?
   A. 16   B. 25   C. 9   D. 7
24._____

25. If you do a fundraiser for charities in your area and raise $500 total, how much would you give to each charity if you were donating equal amounts to 3 of them?
   A. $250.00   B. $167.77   C. $50.00   D. $111.11
25._____

KEY (CORRECT ANSWERS)

1.	D		11.	C
2.	B		12.	B
3.	A		13.	C
4.	C		14.	A
5.	D		15.	C
6.	B		16.	C
7.	D		17.	B
8.	A		18.	B
9.	A		19.	C
10.	D		20.	B

21.	C
22.	B
23.	C
24.	A
25.	B

TEST 3

DIRECTIONS: Each question or incomplete statement is followed by several suggested answers or completions. Select the one that BEST answers the question or completes the statement. *PRINT THE LETTER OF THE CORRECT ANSWER IN THE SPACE AT THE RIGHT.*

Questions 1-3.

DIRECTIONS: In answering Questions 1 through 3, choose the correctly spelled word.

1.   A.   allusion   B. alusion   C. allusien   D. allution   1._____

2.   A.   altitude   B. alltitude   C. atlitude   D. altlitude   2._____

3.   A.   althogh   B. allthough   C. althrough   D. although   3._____

Questions 4-9.

DIRECTIONS: In answering Questions 4 through 9, choose the answer that BEST completes the analogy.

4.   Odometer is to mileage as compass is to   4._____
       A. speed   B. needle   C. hiking   D. direction

5.   Marathon is to race as hibernation is to   5._____
       A. winter   B. dream   C. sleep   D. bear

6.   Cup is to coffee as bowl is to   6._____
       A. dish   B. spoon   C. food   D. soup

7.   Flow is to river as stagnant is to   7._____
       A. pool   B. rain   C. stream   D. canal

8.   Paw is to cat as hoof is to   8._____
       A. lamb   B. horse   C. lion   D. elephant

9.   Architect is to building as sculptor is to   9._____
       A. museum   B. chisel   C. stone   D. statue

Questions 10-14.

DIRECTIONS: Questions 10 through 14 are to be answered on the basis of the following graph.

Population of Carroll City Broken Down by Age and Gender (in Thousands)			
Age	Female	Male	Total
Under 15	60	60	120
15-23		22	
24-33		20	44
34-43	13	18	31
44-53	20		67
64 and Over	65	65	130
TOTAL	230	232	462

10. How many people in the city are between the ages of 15-23?
    A. 70   B. 46,000   C. 70,000   D. 225,000

10.____

11. Approximately what percentage of the total population of the city was female aged 24-33?
    A. 10%   B. 5%   C. 15%   D. 25%

11.____

12. If 33% of the males have a job and 55% of females don't have a job, which of the following statements is TRUE?
    A. Males have approximately 2,600 more jobs than females.
    B. Females have approximately 49,000 more jobs than males.
    C. Females have approximately 26,000 more jobs than males.
    D. None of the above statements are true.

12.____

13. How many females between the ages of 15-23 live in Carroll City?
    A. 67,000   B. 24,000   C. 48,000   D. 91,000

13.____

14. Assume all males 44-53 living in Carroll City are employed. If two-thirds of males age 44-53 work jobs outside of Carroll City, how many work within city limits?
    A. 31,333
    B. 15,667
    C. 47,000
    D. Cannot answer the question with the information provided

14.____

Questions 15-16.

DIRECTIONS: Questions 15 and 16 are labeled as shown. Alphabetize them for filing.
Choose the answer that correctly shows the order.

15. (1) AED   15._____
     (2) OOS
     (3) FOA
     (4) DOM
     (5) COB

    A. 2-5-4-3-2   B. 1-4-5-2-3   C. 1-5-4-2-3   D. 1-5-4-3-2

16. Alphabetize the names of the people. Last names are given last.   16._____
     (1) Lindsey Jamestown
     (2) Jane Alberta
     (3) Ally Jamestown
     (4) Allison Johnston
     (5) Lyle Moreno

    A. 2-1-3-4-5   B. 3-4-2-1-5   C. 2-3-1-4-5   D. 4-3-2-1-5

17. Which of the following words is misspelled?   17._____
    A. disgust   B. whisper
    C. locale   D. none of the above

Questions 18-21.

DIRECTIONS: Questions 18 through 21 are to be answered on the basis of the following list of
employees.

    Robertson, Aaron
    Bacon, Gina
    Jerimiah, Trace
    Gillette, Stanley
    Jacks, Sharon

18. Which employee name would come in third in alphabetized list?   18._____
    A. Robertson, Aaron   B. Jerimiah, Trace
    C. Gillette, Stanley   D. Jacks, Sharon

19. Which employee's first name starts with the letter in the alphabet that is   19._____
     five letters after the first letter of their last name?
    A. Jerimiah, Trace   B. Bacon, Gina
    C. Jacks, Sharon   D. Gillette, Stanley

20. How many employees have last names that are exactly five letters long?   20._____
    A. 1   B. 2   C. 3   D. 4

21. How many of the employees have either a first or last name that starts with the letter "G"?   21.____
    A. 1   B. 2   C. 4   D. 5

Questions 22-25.

DIRECTIONS: Questions 22 through 25 are to be answered on the basis of the following chart.

Bicycle Sales (Model #34JA32)							
Country	May	June	July	August	September	October	Total
Germany	34	47	45	54	56	60	296
Britain	40	44	36	47	47	46	260
Ireland	37	32	32	32	34	33	200
Portugal	14	14	14	16	17	14	89
Italy	29	29	28	31	29	31	177
Belgium	22	24	24	26	25	23	144
Total	176	198	179	206	208	207	1166

22. What percentage of the overall total was sold to the German importer?   22.____
    A. 25.3%   B. 22%   C. 24.1%   D. 23%

23. What percentage of the overall total was sold in September?   23.____
    A. 24.1%   B. 25.6%   C. 17.9%   D. 24.6%

24. What is the average number of units per month imported into Belgium over the first four months shown?   24.____
    A. 26   B. 20   C. 24   D. 31

25. If you look at the three smallest importers, what is their total import percentage?   25.____
    A. 35.1%   B. 37.1%   C. 40%   D. 28%

KEY (CORRECT ANSWERS)

1.	A		11.	B
2.	A		12.	C
3.	D		13.	C
4.	D		14.	B
5.	C		15.	D
6.	D		16.	C
7.	A		17.	D
8.	B		18.	D
9.	D		19.	B
10.	C		20.	B

21. B
22. A
23. C
24. C
25. A

TEST 4

DIRECTIONS: Each question or incomplete statement is followed by several suggested answers or completions. Select the one that BEST answers the question or completes the statement. *PRINT THE LETTER OF THE CORRECT ANSWER IN THE SPACE AT THE RIGHT.*

Questions 1-6.

DIRECTIONS: In answering Questions 1 through 6, choose the sentence that represents the BEST example of English grammar.

1.　A.　Joey and me want to go on a vacation next week.　　　　1.＿＿＿
　　B.　Gary told Jim he would need to take some time off.
　　C.　If turning six years old, Jim's uncle would teach Spanish to him.
　　D.　Fax a copy of your resume to Ms. Perez and me.

2.　A.　Jerry stood in line for almost two hours.　　　　2.＿＿＿
　　B.　The reaction to my engagement was less exciting than I thought it would be.
　　C.　Carlos and me have done great work on this project.
　　D.　Two parts of the speech needs to be revised before tomorrow.

3.　A.　Arriving home, the alarm was tripped.　　　　3.＿＿＿
　　B.　Jonny is regarded as a stand up guy, a responsible parent, and he doesn't give up until a task is finished.
　　C.　Each employee must submit a drug test each month.
　　D.　One of the documents was incinerated in the explosion.

4.　A.　As soon as my parents get home, I told them I finished all of my chores.　　　　4.＿＿＿
　　B.　I asked my teacher to send me my missing work, check my absences, and how did I do on my test.
　　C.　Matt attempted to keep it concealed from Jenny and me.
　　D.　If Mary or him cannot get work done on time, I will have to split them up.

5.　A.　Driving to work, the traffic report warned him of an accident on Highway 47.　　　　5.＿＿＿
　　B.　Jimmy has performed well this season.
　　C.　Since finishing her degree, several job offers have been given to Cam.
　　D.　Our boss is creating unstable conditions for we employees.

6.　A.　The thief was described as a tall man with a wiry mustache weighing approximately 150 pounds.　　　　6.＿＿＿
　　B.　She gave Patrick and I some more time to finish our work.
　　C.　One of the books that he ordered was damaged in shipping.
　　D.　While talking on the rotary phone, the car Jim was driving skidded off the road.

Questions 7-9.

DIRECTIONS: Questions 7 through 9 are to be answered on the basis of the following graph.

Ice Lake Frozen Flight (2002-2013)		
Year	Number of Participants	Temperature (Fahrenheit)
2002	22	4°
2003	50	33°
2004	69	18°
2005	104	22°
2006	108	24°
2007	288	33°
2008	173	9°
2009	598	39°
2010	698	26°
2011	696	30°
2012	777	28°
2013	578	32°

7.   Which two year span had the LARGEST difference between temperatures?   7._____
     A. 2002 and 2003   B. 2011 and 2012
     C. 2008 and 2009   D. 2003 and 2004

8.   How many total people participated in the years after the temperature   8._____
     reached at least 29°?
     A. 2,295   B. 1,717   C. 2,210   D. 4,543

9.   In 2007, the event saw 288 participants, while in 2008 that number   9._____
     dropped to 173. Which of the following reasons BEST explains the drop in
     participants?
     A. The event had not been going on that long and people didn't know about
         it.
     B. The lake water wasn't cold enough to have people jump in.
     C. The temperature was too cold for many people who would have normally
         participated.
     D. None of the above reasons explain the drop in participants.

10. In the following list of numbers, how many times does 4 come just after 2   10._____
     when 2 comes just after an odd number?
     23652476538986324885724863924 24
     A. 2   B. 3   C. 4   D. 5

11. Which choice below lists the letter that is as far after B as S is after N in   11._____
     the alphabet?
     A. G   B. H   C. I   D. J

Questions 12-15.

DIRECTIONS: Questions 12 through 15 are to be answered on the basis of the following directory and list of changes.

Directory		
Name	Emp. Type	Position
Julie Taylor	Warehouse	Packer
James King	Office	Administrative Assistant
John Williams	Office	Salesperson
Ray Moore	Warehouse	Maintenance
Kathleen Byrne	Warehouse	Supervisor
Amy Jones	Office	Salesperson
Paul Jonas	Office	Salesperson
Lisa Wong	Warehouse	Loader
Eugene Lee	Office	Accountant
Bruce Lavine	Office	Manager
Adam Gates	Warehouse	Packer
Will Suter	Warehouse	Packer
Gary Lorper	Office	Accountant
Jon Adams	Office	Salesperson
Susannah Harper	Office	Salesperson

Directory Updates:
- Employee e-mail address will adhere to the following guidelines: lastnamefirstname@apexindustries.com (ex. Susannah Harper is harpersusannah@apexindustries.com). Currently, employees in the warehouse share one e-mail, distribution@apexindustries.com.
- The "Loader" position was now be referred to as "Specialist I"
- Adam Gates has accepted a Supervisor position within the Warehouse and is no longer a Packer. All warehouses employees report to the two Supervisors and all office employees report to the Manager.

12. Amy Jones tried to send an e-mail to Adam Gates, but it wouldn't send. Which of the following offers the BEST explanation?
   A. Amy put Adam's first name first and then his last name.
   B. Adam doesn't check his e-mail, so he wouldn't know if he received the e-mail or not.
   C. Adam does not have his own e-mail.
   D. Office employees are not allowed to send e-mails to each other.

12.____

13. How many Packers currently work for Apex Industries?
   A. 2   B. 3   C. 4   D. 5

13.____

14. What position does Lisa Wong currently hold?
   A. Specialist I   B. Secretary
   C. Administrative Assistant   D. Loader

14.____

15. If an employee wanted to contact the office manager, which of the following e-mails should the e-mail be sent to?
    A. officemanager@apexindustries.com
    B. brucelavine@apexindustries.com
    C. lavinebruce@apexindustries.com
    D. distribution@apexindustries.com

15.____

Questions 16-19.

DIRECTIONS: In answering Questions 16 through 19, compare the three names, numbers or addresses.

16. Smiley Yarnell   Smiley Yarnel   Smily Yarnell   16.____
    A. All three are exactly alike.
    B. The first and second are exactly alike.
    C. The second and third are exactly alike.
    D. All three are different.

17. 1583 Theater Drive   1583 Theater Drive   1583 Theatre Drive   17.____
    A. All three are exactly alike.
    B. The first and second are exactly alike.
    C. The second and third are exactly alike.
    D. All three are different.

18. 3341893212   3341893212   3341893212   18.____
    A. All three are exactly alike.
    B. The first and second are exactly alike.
    C. The second and third are exactly alike.
    D. All three are different.

19. Douglass Watkins   Douglas Watkins   Douglass Watkins   19.____
    A. All three are exactly alike.
    B. The first and third are exactly alike.
    C. The second and third are exactly alike.
    D. All three are different.

Questions 20-24.

DIRECTIONS: In answering Questions 20 through 24, you will be presented with a word. Choose the synonym that BEST represents the word in question.

20. Flexible   20.____
    A. delicate   B. inflammable C. strong   D. pliable

21. Alternative   21.____
    A. choice   B. moderate   C. lazy   D. value

22. Corroborate
    A. examine   B. explain   C. verify   D. explain
22.____

23. Respiration
    A. recovery   B. breathing   C. sweating   D. selfish
23.____

24. Negligent
    A. lazy   B. moderate   C. hopeless   D. lax
24.____

25. Plumber is to Wrench as Painter is to
    A. pipe   B. shop   C. hammer   D. brush
25.____

KEY (CORRECT ANSWERS)

1.	D		11.	A
2.	A		12.	C
3.	D		13.	A
4.	C		14.	A
5.	B		15.	C
6.	C		16.	D
7.	C		17.	B
8.	B		18.	A
9.	C		19.	B
10.	C		20.	D

21.	A
22.	C
23.	B
24.	D
25.	D

PHILOSOPHY, PRINCIPLES, PRACTICES AND TECHNICS
OF
SUPERVISION, ADMINISTRATION, MANAGEMENT AND ORGANIZATION

TABLE OF CONTENTS

Page

I.	MEANING OF SUPERVISION	1
II.	THE OLD AND THE NEW SUPERVISION	1
III.	THE EIGHT (8) BASIC PRINCIPLES OF THE NEW SUPERVISION	1
	1. Principle of Responsibility	1
	2. Principle of Authority	2
	3. Principle of Self-Growth	2
	4. Principle of Individual Worth	2
	5. Principle of Creative Leadership	2
	6. Principle of Success and Failure	2
	7. Principle of Science	3
	8. Principle of Cooperation	3
IV.	WHAT IS ADMINISTRATION?	3
	1. Practices commonly classed as "Supervisory"	3
	2. Practices commonly classed as "Administrative"	3
	3. Practices classified as both "Supervisory" and "Administrative"	4
V.	RESPONSIBILITIES OF THE SUPERVISOR	4
VI.	COMPETENCIES OF THE SUPERVISOR	4
VII.	THE PROFESSIONAL SUPERVISOR—EMPLOYEE RELATIONSHIP	4
VIII.	MINI-TEXT IN SUPERVISION, ADMINISTRATION, MANAGEMENT AND ORGANIZATION	5
	A. Brief Highlights	5
	1. Levels of Management	5
	2. What the Supervisor Must Learn	6
	3. A Definition of Supervision	6
	4. Elements of the Team Concept	6
	5. Principles of Organization	6
	6. The Four Important Parts of Every Job	6
	7. Principles of Delegation	6
	8. Principles of Effective Communications	7
	9. Principles of Work Improvement	7

10.	Areas of Job Improvement	7
11.	Seven Key Points in Making Improvements	7
12.	Corrective Techniques for Job Improvement	7
13.	A Planning Checklist	8
14.	Five Characteristics of Good Directions	8
15.	Types of Directions	8
16.	Controls	8
17.	Orienting the New Employee	8
18.	Checklist for Orienting New Employees	8
19.	Principles of Learning	9
20.	Causes of Poor Performance	9
21.	Four Major Steps in On-The-Job Instructions	9
22.	Employees Want Five Things	9
23.	Some Don'ts in Regard to Praise	9
24.	How to Gain Your Workers' Confidence	9
25.	Sources of Employee Problems	9
26.	The Supervisor's Key to Discipline	10
27.	Five Important Processes of Management	10
28.	When the Supervisor Fails to Plan	10
29.	Fourteen General Principles of Management	10
30.	Change	10

B. Brief Topical Summaries   11

I.	Who/What is the Supervisor?	11
II.	The Sociology of Work	11
III.	Principles and Practices of Supervision	12
IV.	Dynamic Leadership	12
V.	Processes for Solving Problems	12
VI.	Training for Results	13
VII.	Health, Safety and Accident Prevention	13
VIII.	Equal Employment Opportunity	13
IX.	Improving Communications	14
X.	Self-Development	14
XI.	Teaching and Training	14
	A. The Teaching Process	14
	1. Preparation	14
	2. Presentation	15
	3. Summary	15
	4. Application	15
	5. Evaluation	15
	B. Teaching Methods	15
	1. Lecture	15
	2. Discussion	15
	3. Demonstration	16
	4. Performance	16
	5. Which Method to Use	16

PHILOSOPHY, PRINCIPLES, PRACTICES, AND TECHNICS
OF
SUPERVISION, ADMINISTRATION, MANAGEMENT AND ORGANIZATION

I. MEANING OF SUPERVISION

The extension of the democratic philosophy has been accompanied by an extension in the scope of supervision. Modern leaders and supervisors no longer think of supervision in the narrow sense of being confined chiefly to visiting employees, supplying materials, or rating the staff. They regard supervision as being intimately related to all the concerned agencies of society, they speak of the supervisor's function in terms of "growth", rather than the "improvement," of employees.

This modern concept of supervision may be defined as follows:

Supervision is leadership and the development of leadership within groups which are cooperatively engaged in inspection, research, training, guidance and evaluation.

II. THE OLD AND THE NEW SUPERVISION

TRADITIONAL
1. Inspection
2. Focused on the employee
3. Visitation
4. Random and haphazard
5. Imposed and authoritarian
6. One person usually

MODERN
1. Study and analysis
2. Focused on aims, materials, methods, supervisors, employees, environment
3. Demonstrations, intervisitation, workshops, directed reading, bulletins, etc.
4. Definitely organized and planned (scientific)
5. Cooperative and democratic
6. Many persons involved (creative)

III THE EIGHT (8) BASIC PRINCIPLES OF THE NEW SUPERVISION

1. *PRINCIPLE OF RESPONSIBILITY*
Authority to act and responsibility for acting must be joined.
   a. If you give responsibility, give authority.
   b. Define employee duties clearly.
   c. Protect employees from criticism by others.
   d. Recognize the rights as well as obligations of employees.
   e. Achieve the aims of a democratic society insofar as it is possible within the area of your work.
   f. Establish a situation favorable to training and learning.
   g. Accept ultimate responsibility for everything done in your section, unit, office, division, department.
   h. Good administration and good supervision are inseparable.

2. PRINCIPLE OF AUTHORITY
The success of the supervisor is measured by the extent to which the power of authority is not used.

      a. Exercise simplicity and informality in supervision.
      b. Use the simplest machinery of supervision.
      c. If it is good for the organization as a whole, it is probably justified.
      d. Seldom be arbitrary or authoritative.
      e. Do not base your work on the power of position or of personality.
      f. Permit and encourage the free expression of opinions.

3. PRINCIPLE OF SELF-GROWTH
The success of the supervisor is measured by the extent to which, and the speed with which, he is no longer needed.

      a. Base criticism on principles, not on specifics.
      b. Point out higher activities to employees.
      c. Train for self-thinking by employees, to meet new situations.
      d. Stimulate initiative, self-reliance and individual responsibility.
      e. Concentrate on stimulating the growth of employees rather than on removing defects.

4. PRINCIPLE OF INDIVIDUAL WORTH
Respect for the individual is a paramount consideration in supervision.

      a. Be human and sympathetic in dealing with employees.
      b. Don't nag about things to be done.
      c. Recognize the individual differences among employees and seek opportunities to permit best expression of each personality.

5. PRINCIPLE OF CREATIVE LEADERSHIP
The best supervision is that which is not apparent to the employee.

      a. Stimulate, don't drive employees to creative action.
      b. Emphasize doing good things.
      c. Encourage employees to do what they do best.
      d. Do not be too greatly concerned with details of subject or method.
      e. Do not be concerned exclusively with immediate problems and activities.
      f. Reveal higher activities and make them both desired and maximally possible.
      g. Determine procedures in the light of each situation but see that these are derived from a sound basic philosophy.
      h. Aid, inspire and lead so as to liberate the creative spirit latent in all good employees.

6. PRINCIPLE OF SUCCESS AND FAILURE
There are no unsuccessful employees, only unsuccessful supervisors who have failed to give proper leadership.

      a. Adapt suggestions to the capacities, attitudes, and prejudices of employees.
      b. Be gradual, be progressive, be persistent.
      c. Help the employee find the general principle; have the employee apply his own problem to the general principle.
      d. Give adequate appreciation for good work and honest effort.
      e. Anticipate employee difficulties and help to prevent them.
      f. Encourage employees to do the desirable things they will do anyway.
      g. Judge your supervision by the results it secures.

7. *PRINCIPLE OF SCIENCE*

Successful supervision is scientific, objective, and experimental. It is based on facts, not on prejudices.

        a. Be cumulative in results.
        b. Never divorce your suggestions from the goals of training.
        c. Don't be impatient of results.
        d. Keep all matters on a professional, not a personal level.
        e. Do not be concerned exclusively with immediate problems and activities.
        f. Use objective means of determining achievement and rating where possible.

8. *PRINCIPLE OF COOPERATION*

Supervision is a cooperative enterprise between supervisor and employee.

        a. Begin with conditions as they are.
        b. Ask opinions of all involved when formulating policies.
        c. Organization is as good as its weakest link.
        d. Let employees help to determine policies and department programs.
        e. Be approachable and accessible - physically and mentally.
        f. Develop pleasant social relationships.

IV. WHAT IS ADMINISTRATION?

Administration is concerned with providing the environment, the material facilities, and the operational procedures that will promote the maximum growth and development of supervisors and employees. (Organization is an aspect, and a concomitant, of administration.)

There is no sharp line of demarcation between supervision and administration; these functions are intimately interrelated and, often, overlapping. They are complementary activities.

1. *PRACTICES COMMONLY CLASSED AS "SUPERVISORY"*

        a. Conducting employees conferences
        b. Visiting sections, units, offices, divisions, departments
        c. Arranging for demonstrations
        d. Examining plans
        e. Suggesting professional reading
        f. Interpreting bulletins
        g. Recommending in-service training courses
        h. Encouraging experimentation
        i. Appraising employee morale
        j. Providing for intervisitation

2. *PRACTICES COMMONLY CLASSIFIED AS "ADMINISTRATIVE"*

        a. Management of the office
        b. Arrangement of schedules for extra duties
        c. Assignment of rooms or areas
        d. Distribution of supplies
        e. Keeping records and reports
        f. Care of audio-visual materials
        g. Keeping inventory records
        h. Checking record cards and books
        i. Programming special activities
        j. Checking on the attendance and punctuality of employees

3. *PRACTICES COMMONLY CLASSIFIED AS BOTH "SUPERVISORY" AND "ADMINISTRATIVE"*
    a. Program construction
    b. Testing or evaluating outcomes
    c. Personnel accounting
    d. Ordering instructional materials

V. RESPONSIBILITIES OF THE SUPERVISOR

A person employed in a supervisory capacity must constantly be able to improve his own efficiency and ability. He represents the employer to the employees and only continuous self-examination can make him a capable supervisor.

Leadership and training are the supervisor's responsibility. An efficient working unit is one in which the employees work with the supervisor. It is his job to bring out the best in his employees. He must always be relaxed, courteous and calm in his association with his employees. Their feelings are important, and a harsh attitude does not develop the most efficient employees.

VI. COMPETENCIES OF THE SUPERVISOR

1. Complete knowledge of the duties and responsibilities of his position.
2. To be able to organize a job, plan ahead and carry through.
3. To have self-confidence and initiative.
4. To be able to handle the unexpected situation and make quick decisions.
5. To be able to properly train subordinates in the positions they are best suited for.
6. To be able to keep good human relations among his subordinates.
7. To be able to keep good human relations between his subordinates and himself and to earn their respect and trust.

VII. THE PROFESSIONAL SUPERVISOR-EMPLOYEE RELATIONSHIP

There are two kinds of efficiency: one kind is only apparent and is produced in organizations through the exercise of mere discipline; this is but a simulation of the second, or true, efficiency which springs from spontaneous cooperation. If you are a manager, no matter how great or small your responsibility, it is your job, in the final analysis, to create and develop this involuntary cooperation among the people whom you supervise. For, no matter how powerful a combination of money, machines, and materials a company may have, this is a dead and sterile thing without a team of willing, thinking and articulate people to guide it.

The following 21 points are presented as indicative of the exemplary basic relationship that should exist between supervisor and employee:

1. Each person wants to be liked and respected by his fellow employee and wants to be treated with consideration and respect by his superior.
2. The most competent employee will make an error. However, in a unit where good relations exist between the supervisor and his employees, tenseness and fear do not exist. Thus, errors are not hidden or covered up and the efficiency of a unit is not impaired.
3. Subordinates resent rules, regulations, or orders that are unreasonable or unexplained.
4. Subordinates are quick to resent unfairness, harshness, injustices and favoritism.
5. An employee will accept responsibility if he knows that he will be complimented for a job well done, and not too harshly chastised for failure; that his supervisor will check the cause of the failure, and, if it was the supervisor's fault, he will assume the blame therefore. If it was the employee's fault, his supervisor will explain the correct method or means of handling the responsibility.

6. An employee wants to receive credit for a suggestion he has made, that is used. If a suggestion cannot be used, the employee is entitled to an explanation. The supervisor should not say "no" and close the subject.
7. Fear and worry slow up a worker's ability. Poor working environment can impair his physical and mental health. A good supervisor avoids forceful methods, threats and arguments to get a job done.
8. A forceful supervisor is able to train his employees individually and as a team, and is able to motivate them in the proper channels.
9. A mature supervisor is able to properly evaluate his subordinates and to keep them happy and satisfied.
10. A sensitive supervisor will never patronize his subordinates.
11. A worthy supervisor will respect his employees' confidences.
12. Definite and clear-cut responsibilities should be assigned to each executive.
13. Responsibility should always be coupled with corresponding authority.
14. No change should be made in the scope or responsibilities of a position without a definite understanding to that effect on the part of all persons concerned.
15. No executive or employee, occupying a single position in the organization, should be subject to definite orders from more than one source.
16. Orders should never be given to subordinates over the head of a responsible executive. Rather than do this, the officer in question should be supplanted.
17. Criticisms of subordinates should, whoever possible, be made privately, and in no case should a subordinate be criticized in the presence of executives or employees of equal or lower rank.
18. No dispute or difference between executives or employees as to authority or responsibilities should be considered too trivial for prompt and careful adjudication.
19. Promotions, wage changes, and disciplinary action should always be approved by the executive immediately superior to the one directly responsible.
20. No executive or employee should ever be required, or expected, to be at the same time an assistant to, and critic of, another.
21. Any executive whose work is subject to regular inspection should, whever practicable, be given the assistance and facilities necessary to enable him to maintain an independent check of the quality of his work.

VIII. MINI-TEXT IN SUPERVISION, ADMINISTRATION, MANAGEMENT, AND ORGANIZATION

A. BRIEF HIGHLIGHTS

Listed concisely and sequentially are major headings and important data in the field for quick recall and review.

1. LEVELS OF MANAGEMENT

Any organization of some size has several levels of management. In terms of a ladder the levels are:

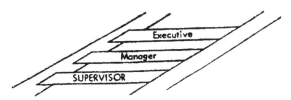

The first level is very important because it is the beginning point of management leadership.

2. WHAT THE SUPERVISOR MUST LEARN

A supervisor must learn to:
(1) Deal with people and their differences
(2) Get the job done through people
(3) Recognize the problems when they exist
(4) Overcome obstacles to good performance
(5) Evaluate the performance of people
(6) Check his own performance in terms of accomplishment

3. A DEFINITION OF SUPERVISOR

The term supervisor means any individual having authority, in the interests of the employer, to hire, transfer, suspend, lay-off, recall, promote, discharge, assign, reward, or discipline other employees or responsibility to direct them, or to adjust their grievances, or effectively to recommend such action, if, in connection with the foregoing, exercise of such authority is not of a merely routine or clerical nature but requires the use of independent judgment.

4. ELEMENTS OF THE TEAM CONCEPT

What is involved in teamwork? The component parts are:

(1) Members	(3) Goals	(5) Cooperation
(2) A leader	(4) Plans	(6) Spirit

5. PRINCIPLES OF ORGANIZATION

(1) A team member must know what his job is.
(2) Be sure that the nature and scope of a job are understood.
(3) Authority and responsibility should be carefully spelled out.
(4) A supervisor should be permitted to make the maximum number of decisions affecting his employees.
(5) Employees should report to only one supervisor.
(6) A supervisor should direct only as many employees as he can handle effectively.
(7) An organization plan should be flexible.
(8) Inspection and performance of work should be separate.
(9) Organizational problems should receive immediate attention.
(10) Assign work in line with ability and experience.

6. THE FOUR IMPORTANT PARTS OF EVERY JOB

(1) Inherent in every job is the *accountability* for results.
(2) A second set of factors in every job is *responsibilities.*
(3) Along with duties and responsibilities one must have the *authority* to act within certain limits without obtaining permission to proceed.
(4) No job exists in a vacuum. The supervisor is surrounded by key *relationships.*

7. PRINCIPLES OF DELEGATION

Where work is delegated for the first time, the supervisor should think in terms of these questions:
(1) Who is best qualified to do this?
(2) Can an employee improve his abilities by doing this?
(3) How long should an employee spend on this?
(4) Are there any special problems for which he will need guidance?
(5) How broad a delegation can I make?

8. PRINCIPLES OF EFFECTIVE COMMUNICATIONS
(1) Determine the media
(2) To whom directed?
(3) Identification and source authority
(4) Is communication understood?

9. PRINCIPLES OF WORK IMPROVEMENT
(1) Most people usually do only the work which is assigned to them
(2) Workers are likely to fit assigned work into the time available to perform it
(3) A good workload usually stimulates output
(4) People usually do their best work when they know that results will be reviewed or inspected
(5) Employees usually feel that someone else is responsible for conditions of work, workplace layout, job methods, type of tools/equipment, and other such factors
(6) Employees are usually defensive about their job security
(7) Employees have natural resistance to change
(8) Employees can support or destroy a supervisor
(9) A supervisor usually earns the respect of his people through his personal example of diligence and efficiency

10. AREAS OF JOB IMPROVEMENT
The areas of job improvement are quite numerous, but the most common ones which a supervisor can identify and utilize are:
(1) Departmental layout
(2) Flow of work
(3) Workplace layout
(4) Utilization of manpower
(5) Work methods
(6) Materials handling
(7) Utilization
(8) Motion economy

11. SEVEN KEY POINTS IN MAKING IMPROVEMENTS
(1) Select the job to be improved
(2) Study how it is being done now
(3) Question the present method
(4) Determine actions to be taken
(5) Chart proposed method
(6) Get approval and apply
(7) Solicit worker participation

12. CORRECTIVE TECHNIQUES OF JOB IMPROVEMENT

Specific Problems	General Improvement	Corrective Techniques
(1) Size of workload	(1) Departmental layout	(1) Study with scale model
(2) Inability to meet schedules	(2) Flow of work	(2) Flow chart study
(3) Strain and fatigue	(3) Work plan layout	(3) Motion analysis
(4) Improper use of men and skills	(4) Utilization of manpower	(4) Comparison of units produced to standard allowance
(5) Waste, poor quality, unsafe conditions	(5) Work methods	(5) Methods analysis
(6) Bottleneck conditions that hinder output	(6) Materials handling	(6) Flow chart & equipment study
(7) Poor utilization of equipment and machine	(7) Utilization of equipment	(7) Down time vs. running time
(8) Efficiency and productivity of labor	(8) Motion economy	(8) Motion analysis

13. A *PLANNING CHECKLIST*
(1) Objectives
(2) Controls
(3) Delegations
(4) Communications
(5) Resources

(6) Resources
(7) Manpower
(8) Equipment
(9) Supplies and materials
(10) Utilization of time

(11) Safety
(12) Money
(13) Work
(14) Timing of improvements

14. *FIVE CHARACTERISTICS OF GOOD DIRECTIONS*
In order to get results, directions must be:
(1) Possible of accomplishment
(2) Agreeable with worker interests
(3) Related to mission
(4) Planned and complete
(5) Unmistakably clear

15. *TYPES OF DIRECTIONS*
(1) Demands or direct orders
(2) Requests
(3) Suggestion or implication
(4) Volunteering

16. *CONTROLS*
A typical listing of the overall areas in which the supervisor should establish controls might be:
(1) Manpower
(2) Materials
(3) Quality of work
(4) Quantity of work
(5) Time
(6) Space
(7) Money
(8) Methods

17. *ORIENTING THE NEW EMPLOYEE*
(1) Prepare for him
(2) Welcome the new employee
(3) Orientation for the job
(4) Follow-up

18. *CHECKLIST FOR ORIENTING NEW EMPLOYEES* Yes No
(1) Do your appreciate the feelings of new employees when they first report for work? ___ ___
(2) Are you aware of the fact that the new employee must make a big adjustment to his job? ___ ___
(3) Have you given him good reasons for liking the job and the organization? ___ ___
(4) Have you prepared for his first day on the job?
(5) Did you welcome him cordially and make him feel needed?
(6) Did you establish rapport with him so that he feels free to talk and discuss matters with you? ___ ___
(7) Did you explain his job to him and his relationship to you? ___ ___
(8) Does he know that his work will be evaluated periodically on a basis that is fair and objective? ___ ___
(9) Did you introduce him to his fellow workers in such a way that they are likely to accept him? ___ ___
(10) Does he know what employee benefits he will receive?
(11) Does he understand the importance of being on the job and what to do if he must leave his duty station? ___ ___
(12) Has he been impressed with the importance of accident prevention and safe practice? ___ ___
(13) Does he generally know his way around the department? ___ ___
(14) Is he under the guidance of a sponsor who will teach the right ways of doing things? ___ ___
(15) Do you plan to follow-up so that he will continue to adjust successfully to his job? ___ ___

19. *PRINCIPLES OF LEARNING*
   (1) Motivation   (2) Demonstration or explanation   (3) Practice

20. *CAUSES OF POOR PERFORMANCE*
   (1) Improper training for job
   (2) Wrong tools
   (3) Inadequate directions
   (4) Lack of supervisory follow-up
   (5) Poor communications
   (6) Lack of standards of performance
   (7) Wrong work habits
   (8) Low morale
   (9) Other

21. *FOUR MAJOR STEPS IN ON-THE-JOB INSTRUCTION*
   (1) Prepare the worker
   (2) Present the operation
   (3) Tryout performance
   (4) Follow-up

22. *EMPLOYEES WANT FIVE THINGS*
   (1) Security   (2) Opportunity   (3) Recognition   (4) Inclusion   (5) Expression

23. *SOME DON'TS IN REGARD TO PRAISE*
   (1) Don't praise a person for something he hasn't done
   (2) Don't praise a person unless you can be sincere
   (3) Don't be sparing in praise just because your superior withholds it from you
   (4) Don't let too much time elapse between good performance and recognition of it

24. *HOW TO GAIN YOUR WORKERS' CONFIDENCE*
   Methods of developing confidence include such things as:
   (1) Knowing the interests, habits, hobbies of employees
   (2) Admitting your own inadequacies
   (3) Sharing and telling of confidence in others
   (4) Supporting people when they are in trouble
   (5) Delegating matters that can be well handled
   (6) Being frank and straightforward about problems and working conditions
   (7) Encouraging others to bring their problems to you
   (8) Taking action on problems which impede worker progress

25. *SOURCES OF EMPLOYEE PROBLEMS*
   On-the-job causes might be such things as:
   (1) A feeling that favoritism is exercised in assignments
   (2) Assignment of overtime
   (3) An undue amount of supervision
   (4) Changing methods or systems
   (5) Stealing of ideas or trade secrets
   (6) Lack of interest in job
   (7) Threat of reduction in force
   (8) Ignorance or lack of communications
   (9) Poor equipment
   (10) Lack of knowing how supervisor feels toward employee
   (11) Shift assignments

   Off-the-job problems might have to do with:
   (1) Health   (2) Finances   (3) Housing   (4) Family

26. *THE SUPERVISOR'S KEY TO DISCIPLINE*

There are several key points about discipline which the supervisor should keep in mind:

   (1) Job discipline is one of the disciplines of life and is directed by the supervisor.

   (2) It is more important to correct an employee fault than to fix blame for it.

   (3) Employee performance is affected by problems both on the job and off.

   (4) Sudden or abrupt changes in behavior can be indications of important employee problems.

   (5) Problems should be dealt with as soon as possible after they are identified.

   (6) The attitude of the supervisor may have more to do with solving problems than the techniques of problem solving.

   (7) Correction of employee behavior should be resorted to only after the supervisor is sure that training or counseling will not be helpful.

   (8) Be sure to document your disciplinary actions.

   (9) Make sure that you are disciplining on the basis of facts rather than personal feelings.

  (10) Take each disciplinary step in order, being careful not to make snap judgments, or decisions based on impatience.

27. *FIVE IMPORTANT PROCESSES OF MANAGEMENT*

   (1) Planning   (2) Organizing   (3) Scheduling

   (4) Controlling   (5) Motivating

28. *WHEN THE SUPERVISOR FAILS TO PLAN*

   (1) Supervisor creates impression of not knowing his job

   (2) May lead to excessive overtime

   (3) Job runs itself -- supervisor lacks control

   (4) Deadlines and appointments missed

   (5) Parts of the work go undone

   (6) Work interrupted by emergencies

   (7) Sets a bad example

   (8) Uneven workload creates peaks and valleys

   (9) Too much time on minor details at expense of more important tasks

29. *FOURTEEN GENERAL PRINCIPLES OF MANAGEMENT*

   (1) Division of work   (8) Centralization

   (2) Authority and responsibility   (9) Scalar chain

   (3) Discipline   (10) Order

   (4) Unity of command   (11) Equity

   (5) Unity of direction   (12) Stability of tenure of

   (6) Subordination of individual   personnel

       interest to general interest   (13) Initiative

   (7) Remuneration of personnel   (14) Esprit de corps

30. *CHANGE*

Bringing about change is perhaps attempted more often, and yet less well understood, than anything else the supervisor does. How do people generally react to change? (People tend to resist change that is imposed upon them by other individuals or circumstances.

Change is characteristic of every situation. It is a part of every real endeavor where the efforts of people are concerned.

A. Why do people resist change?
   People may resist change because of:
      (1) Fear of the unknown
      (2) Implied criticism
      (3) Unpleasant experiences in the past
      (4) Fear of loss of status
      (5) Threat to the ego
      (6) Fear of loss of economic stability

B. How can we best overcome the resistance to change?
   In initiating change, take these steps:
      (1) Get ready to sell
      (2) Identify sources of help
      (3) Anticipate objections
      (4) Sell benefits
      (5) Listen in depth
      (6) Follow up

B. BRIEF TOPICAL SUMMARIES

I. WHO/WHAT IS THE SUPERVISOR?
1. The supervisor is often called the "highest level employee and the lowest level manager."
2. A supervisor is a member of both management and the work group. He acts as a bridge between the two.
3. Most problems in supervision are in the area of human relations, or people problems.
4. Employees expect: Respect, opportunity to learn and to advance, and a sense of belonging, and so forth.
5. Supervisors are responsible for directing people and organizing work. Planning is of paramount importance.
6. A position description is a set of duties and responsibilities inherent to a given position.
7. It is important to keep the position description up-to-date and to provide each employee with his own copy.

II. THE SOCIOLOGY OF WORK
1. People are alike in many ways; however, each individual is unique.
2. The supervisor is challenged in getting to know employee differences. Acquiring skills in evaluating individuals is an asset.
3. Maintaining meaningful working relationships in the organization is of great importance.
4. The supervisor has an obligation to help individuals to develop to their fullest potential.
5. Job rotation on a planned basis helps to build versatility and to maintain interest and enthusiasm in work groups.
6. Cross training (job rotation) provides backup skills.
7. The supervisor can help reduce tension by maintaining a sense of humor, providing guidance to employees, and by making reasonable and timely decisions. Employees respond favorably to working under reasonably predictable circumstances.
8. Change is characteristic of all managerial behavior. The supervisor must adjust to changes in procedures, new methods, technological changes, and to a number of new and sometimes challenging situations.
9. To overcome the natural tendency for people to resist change, the supervisor should become more skillful in initiating change.

III. PRINCIPLES AND PRACTICES OF SUPERVISION

1. Employees should be required to answer to only one superior.
2. A supervisor can effectively direct only a limited number of employees, depending upon the complexity, variety, and proximity of the jobs involved.
3. The organizational chart presents the organization in graphic form. It reflects lines of authority and responsibility as well as interrelationships of units within the organization.
4. Distribution of work can be improved through an analysis using the "Work Distribution Chart."
5. The "Work Distribution Chart" reflects the division of work within a unit in understandable form.
6. When related tasks are given to an employee, he has a better chance of increasing his skills through training.
7. The individual who is given the responsibility for tasks must also be given the appropriate authority to insure adequate results.
8. The supervisor should delegate repetitive, routine work. Preparation of recurring reports, maintaining leave and attendance records are some examples.
9. Good discipline is essential to good task performance. Discipline is reflected in the actions of employees on the job in the absence of supervision.
10. Disciplinary action may have to be taken when the positive aspects of discipline have failed. Reprimand, warning, and suspension are examples of disciplinary action.
11. If a situation calls for a reprimand, be sure it is deserved and remember it is to be done in private.

IV. DYNAMIC LEADERSHIP

1. A style is a personal method or manner of exerting influence.
2. Authoritarian leaders often see themselves as the source of power and authority.
3. The democratic leader often perceives the group as the source of authority and power.
4. Supervisors tend to do better when using the pattern of leadership that is most natural for them.
5. Social scientists suggest that the effective supervisor use the leadership style that best fits the problem or circumstances involved.
6. All four styles -- telling, selling, consulting, joining -- have their place. Using one does not preclude using the other at another time.
7. The theory X point of view assumes that the average person dislikes work, will avoid it whenever possible, and must be coerced to achieve organizational objectives.
8. The theory Y point of view assumes that the average person considers work to be as natural as play, and, when the individual is committed, he requires little supervision or direction to accomplish desired objectives.
9. The leader's basic assumptions concerning human behavior and human nature affect his actions, decisions, and other managerial practices.
10. Dissatisfaction among employees is often present, but difficult to isolate. The supervisor should seek to weaken dissatisfaction by keeping promises, being sincere and considerate, keeping employees informed, and so forth.
11. Constructive suggestions should be encouraged during the natural progress of the work.

V. PROCESSES FOR SOLVING PROBLEMS

1. People find their daily tasks more meaningful and satisfying when they can improve them.
2. The causes of problems, or the key factors, are often hidden in the background. Ability to solve problems often involves the ability to isolate them from their backgrounds. There is some substance to the cliché that some persons "can't see the forest for the trees."
3. New procedures are often developed from old ones. Problems should be broken down into manageable parts. New ideas can be adapted from old ones.

4. People think differently in problem-solving situations. Using a logical, patterned approach is often useful. One approach found to be useful includes these steps:

    (a) Define the problem   (d) Weigh and decide
    (b) Establish objectives   (e) Take action
    (c) Get the facts   (f) Evaluate action

VI. TRAINING FOR RESULTS

1. Participants respond best when they feel training is important to them.
2. The supervisor has responsibility for the training and development of those who report to him.
3. When training is delegated to others, great care must be exercised to insure the trainer has knowledge, aptitude, and interest for his work as a trainer.
4. Training (learning) of some type goes on continually. The most successful supervisor makes certain the learning contributes in a productive manner to operational goals.
5. New employees are particularly susceptible to training. Older employees facing new job situations require specific training, as well as having need for development and growth opportunities.
6. Training needs require continuous monitoring.
7. The training officer of an agency is a professional with a responsibility to assist supervisors in solving training problems.
8. Many of the self-development steps important to the supervisor's own growth are equally important to the development of peers and subordinates. Knowledge of these is important when the supervisor consults with others on development and growth opportunities.

VII. HEALTH, SAFETY, AND ACCIDENT PREVENTION

1. Management-minded supervisors take appropriate measures to assist employees in maintaining health and in assuring safe practices in the work environment.
2. Effective safety training and practices help to avoid injury and accidents.
3. Safety should be a management goal. All infractions of safety which are observed should be corrected without exception.
4. Employees' safety attitude, training and instruction, provision of safe tools and equipment, supervision, and leadership are considered highly important factors which contribute to safety and which can be influenced directly by supervisors.
5. When accidents do occur they should be investigated promptly for very important reasons, including the fact that information which is gained can be used to prevent accidents in the future.

VIII. EQUAL EMPLOYMENT OPPORTUNITY

1. The supervisor should endeavor to treat all employees fairly, without regard to religion, race, sex, or national origin.
2. Groups tend to reflect the attitude of the leader. Prejudice can be detected even in very subtle form. Supervisors must strive to create a feeling of mutual respect and confidence in every employee.
3. Complete utilization of all human resources is a national goal. Equitable consideration should be accorded women in the work force, minority-group members, the physically and mentally handicapped, and the older employee. The important question is: "Who can do the job?"
4. Training opportunities, recognition for performance, overtime assignments, promotional opportunities, and all other personnel actions are to be handled on an equitable basis.

IX. IMPROVING COMMUNICATIONS

1. Communications is achieving understanding between the sender and the receiver of a message. It also means sharing information -- the creation of understanding.
2. Communication is basic to all human activity. Words are means of conveying meanings; however, real meanings are in people.
3. There are very practical differences in the effectiveness of one-way, impersonal, and two-way communications. Words spoken face-to-face are better understood. Telephone conversations are effective, but lack the rapport of person-to-person exchanges. The whole person communicates.
4. Cooperation and communication in an organization go hand in hand. When there is a mutual respect between people, spelling out rules and procedures for communicating is unnecessary.
5. There are several barriers to effective communications. These include failure to listen with respect and understanding, lack of skill in feedback, and misinterpreting the meanings of words used by the speaker. It is also common practice to listen to what we want to hear, and tune out things we do not want to hear.
6. Communication is management's chief problem. The supervisor should accept the challenge to communicate more effectively and to improve interagency and intra-agency communications.
7. The supervisor may often plan for and conduct meetings. The planning phase is critical and may determine the success or the failure of a meeting.
8. Speaking before groups usually requires extra effort. Stage fright may never disappear completely, but it can be controlled.

X. SELF-DEVELOPMENT

1. Every employee is responsible for his own self-development.
2. Toastmaster and toastmistress clubs offer opportunities to improve skills in oral communications.
3. Planning for one's own self-development is of vital importance. Supervisors know their own strengths and limitations better than anyone else.
4. Many opportunities are open to aid the supervisor in his developmental efforts, including job assignments; training opportunities, both governmental and non-governmental -- to include universities and professional conferences and seminars.
5. Programmed instruction offers a means of studying at one's own rate.
6. Where difficulties may arise from a supervisor's being away from his work for training, he may participate in televised home study or correspondence courses to meet his self-develop- ment needs.

XI. TEACHING AND TRAINING

A. The Teaching Process

Teaching is encouraging and guiding the learning activities of students toward established goals. In most cases this process consists in five steps: preparation, presentation, summarization, evaluation, and application.

1. Preparation

Preparation is twofold in nature; that of the supervisor and the employee.

Preparation by the supervisor is absolutely essential to success. He must know what, when, where, how, and whom he will teach. Some of the factors that should be considered are:

(1) The objectives
(2) The materials needed
(3) The methods to be used
(4) Employee participation
(5) Employee interest
(6) Training aids
(7) Evaluation
(8) Summarization

Employee preparation consists in preparing the employee to receive the material. Probably the most important single factor in the preparation of the employee is arousing and maintaining his interest. He must know the objectives of the training, why he is there, how the material can be used, and its importance to him.

2. Presentation

In presentation, have a carefully designed plan and follow it.
The plan should be accurate and complete, yet flexible enough to meet situations as they arise. The method of presentation will be determined by the particular situation and objectives.

3. Summary

A summary should be made at the end of every training unit and program. In addition, there may be internal summaries depending on the nature of the material being taught. The important thing is that the trainee must always be able to understand how each part of the new material relates to the whole.

4. Application

The supervisor must arrange work so the employee will be given a chance to apply new knowledge or skills while the material is still clear in his mind and interest is high. The trainee does not really know whether he has learned the material until he has been given a chance to apply it. If the material is not applied, it loses most of its value.

5. Evaluation

The purpose of all training is to promote learning. To determine whether the training has been a success or failure, the supervisor must evaluate this learning.

In the broadest sense evaluation includes all the devices, methods, skills, and techniques used by the supervisor to keep him self and the employees informed as to their progress toward the objectives they are pursuing. The extent to which the employee has mastered the knowledge, skills, and abilities, or changed his attitudes, as determined by the program objectives, is the extent to which instruction has succeeded or failed.

Evaluation should not be confined to the end of the lesson, day, or program but should be used continuously. We shall note later the way this relates to the rest of the teaching process.

B. Teaching Methods

A teaching method is a pattern of identifiable student and instructor activity used in presenting training material.
All supervisors are faced with the problem of deciding which method should be used at a given time.
As with all methods, there are certain advantages and disadvantages to each method.

1. Lecture

The lecture is direct oral presentation of material by the supervisor. The present trend is to place less emphasis on the trainer's activity and more on that of the trainee.

2. Discussion

Teaching by discussion or conference involves using questions and other techniques to arouse interest and focus attention upon certain areas, and by doing so creating a learning situation. This can be one of the most valuable methods because it gives the employees 'an opportunity to express their ideas and pool their knowledge.

3. Demonstration

The demonstration is used to teach how something works or how to do something. It can be used to show a principle or what the results of a series of actions will be. A well-staged demonstration is particularly effective because it shows proper methods of performance in a realistic manner.

4. Performance

Performance is one of the most fundamental of all learning techniques or teaching methods. The trainee may be able to tell how a specific operation should be performed but he cannot be sure he knows how to perform the operation until he has done so.

5. Which Method to Use

Moreover, there are other methods and techniques of teaching. It is difficult to use any method without other methods entering into it. In any learning situation a combination of methods is usually more effective than anyone method alone.

Finally, evaluation must be integrated into the other aspects of the teaching-learning process.
It must be used in the motivation of the trainees; it must be used to assist in developing understanding during the training; and it must be related to employee application of the results of training.
This is distinctly the role of the supervisor.

———